World of Art

Sir Roland Penrose was born in
and at Cambridge University. Fi
in France, painting and becomi
painters and poets. After returr
the International Surrealist Exhi
painted and exhibited in Londo
Group. After the Second World War (during which he served
as a War Office Lecturer in camouflage) he became one of the
founders of the Institute of Contemporary Arts in London, of
which for many years he was President. He also served on the
British Council and the Arts Council, and as a Trustee of the
Tate Gallery. He died in 1984, a few months after his friend Joan
Miró. Roland Penrose's publications include *Picasso: His Life
and Work, Man Ray, Tàpies* and *Scrapbook 1900–1981*.

Antony Penrose is the son of Roland Penrose and Lee Miller. He
grew up at Farley Farm House in Chiddingly, Sussex, where he
is now Co-Director of the Lee Miller Archives and The Penrose
Collection. Antony Penrose has written numerous books,
articles and two plays, including *Roland Penrose, The Friendly
Surrealist* (2001), *The Lives of Lee Miller* (2012), *The Boy Who
Bit Picasso* (2010) – a children's story about his own childhood
friendship with Picasso – and *Miró and the Magic Animals*
(2016). He is an artist and filmmaker, as well as a curator and
lecturer, and has numerous broadcasting credits to his name.

Eduardo de Benito worked for many years in London as a
broadcaster and features presenter for the BBC World Service,
and as a London correspondent for Spanish political weeklies.
The son of Spanish exiles from Franco's regime, he was
brought up in Bogotá, Mexico City and Paris. He is the author
of two books in Spanish and his first novel in English, *Only a
Little Protocol*, was published in 2011. *Central American and
Caribbean Short Stories* was published in 2014.

1 Joan Miró with the ceramic *Green Woman*, 1968

Miró
Roland Penrose

Third edition
With a foreword by Antony Penrose and
an epilogue by Eduardo de Benito

World of Art

First published in 1970 in the United Kingdom
by Thames & Hudson Ltd, 181A High Holborn,
London WC1V 7QX

www.thamesandhudson.com

First published in 1970 in the United States
of America by Thames & Hudson Inc.,
500 Fifth Avenue, New York, New York 10110

www.thamesandhudsonusa.com

This new edition 2022

Miró © 1970, 1985 and 2022
Thames & Hudson Ltd, London

Text by Roland Penrose
Foreword by Antony Penrose
Epilogue by Eduardo de Benito

Art direction and series design by Kummer & Herrman
Layout by Adam Hay Studio

British Library Cataloguing-in-Publication Data
A catalogue record for this book is available from the
British Library

Library of Congress Control Number 2021943690

ISBN 978-0-500-20479-5

Printed and bound in China through Asia Pacific
Offset Ltd

MIX
Paper from
responsible sources
FSC® C136333
FSC
www.fsc.org

Contents

Foreword

Antony Penrose

So many key friendships leave little trace of when and how they began, and this is particularly true among the informal socializing of the avant-garde in the early years of the twentieth century. My father, Roland Penrose, and Joan Miró probably first met in 1928. Roland had been living in France since 1922 as a young painter and his early work was strongly influenced by meeting Georges Braque. In going to Paris, he had followed the advice of Roger Fry and it was further Bloomsbury influence that prompted him to go and live in Cassis on the Provence coast. Here he met and married Valentine Boué, a surrealist poet already known to Paul Eluard and André Breton. By 1928 they both felt the need to explore the excitement surrealism offered and they bought a flat in Paris, at 8 rue des Saints-Pères on the Rive Gauche, opposite the Louvre. Roland wanted a studio and hearing Max Ernst was about to vacate his, he went to see it.

Roland later wrote:

On my arrival at the rue Tourlaque, Montmartre, with Valentine, we were greatly intrigued by the personality of this blue-eyed young hawk and the paintings from a new world hanging on his studio walls. Among others there was a large white canvas with a message which struck me unforgettably by the simplicity and directness of its union between image and words. Written in a calligraphy that seemed reminiscent of the names painted by Spanish peasants on their carts was the word Photo *followed by* Ceci est la couleur de mes rêves *and a large splash of blue on white virgin canvas....It took years for me to find out that the painting of the colour of his dreams was in fact by Miró, at that time Max's next-door neighbour.*[1]

33

2 Joan Miró and
Roland Penrose,
Majorca, 1970
(photographed by
Lee Miller)

Roland must have been aware of Miró's work and may have
seen images published in André Breton's July 1925 issue of *La
Révolution surrealiste*. How he met Miró, who was notoriously
private to the point of being reclusive, remains unknown but
certainly a friendship developed, perhaps through Max Ernst.
Later Roland was to acquire some important paintings by
Miró, first through his acquisition of the Belgian collector René
Gaffé's collection and then the Eluard collection. Living at
close quarters with *Maternity* (1924), *Head of a Catalan Peasant*
(1925) and *Homage to Nusch* (c. 1936) must have immeasurably
heightened Roland's appreciation of Miró's work.

Perhaps the early friendship was deepened when Roland
went to Barcelona in 1936 to gather information in support of
the Republican forces in the Spanish Civil War. In 1938 Miró
wrote to Roland asking him to help two of his friends, Antonio
Lamolla and Enrique Crous Vidal, held in concentration camps
in Spain.[2] Roland sent money and guarantees.[3] A letter from
Vidal in 1946 indicates that he, at least, survived.[4] A hatred of
Franco in particular and Fascism in general served to unite
these two gentle and profound men. Miró, enigmatic and
deeply spiritual, painted some of the most violent pictures
known. Roland, a Quaker pacifist, later joined the British Army.
The extreme nature of their actions shows us how passionately
they stood for peace, freedom and justice.

Roland's biography of Miró was published in 1970, while Franco was still in power so direct references to the artist's politics had to be carefully excluded to avoid getting Miró in trouble with the Spanish Guardia Civil. Franco died in 1975 and very quickly Miró's anti-Fascist feelings found a very public expression through his collaboration with La Claca, a Catalan theatre group led by Joan Baixas and Teresa Calafell. Miró designed the costumes for their fabulous production, *Mori el Merma* (Death to the Monster). The most ghastly monster of all was a vast Ubu Roi figure representing Franco, a bulbous slobbery giant dripping with gore, simultaneously absurd and threatening. Franco's wife was played by a woman wearing an impossibly long false nose, surrounded by violent acolytes of the monster who chaotically persecuted five sensitive and vulnerable ferrets, representing the oppressed people.

143, 144

The work premiered in 1978 in Palma de Mallorca; Barcelona and a world tour followed, which to Roland's delight included Riverside Studios, London. By this time, Roland had extensively interviewed Miró for a BBC2 documentary titled *Miró and the Theatre of Dreams*, directed by Robin Lough. Miró was wonderfully cooperative, allowing John Hooper the cameraman the intimacy of extreme closeups of his brushwork that convey the intensity with which he worked. Towards the end of the production, the producer Christopher Martin flew to Majorca to show Miró and his wife Pilar the rough cut which, due to technical constraints, had to be projected mute. To their horror Miró was greatly upset by the inclusion of images of the now dead Franco. They were intended to demonstrate what Miró was rebelling against but, without the commentary, he misinterpreted them as implying he admired the Franco regime. It was an anxious moment for Martin, but he managed to convince Miró of the true intention. On release, to everyone's delight, the *Mori el Merma* monsters populated the film, with the ferrets seen climbing on the jagged rocks of the coast. Miró's intimate collaboration with the performers was well portrayed, and Roland's questions and commentary took us backstage of the theatre and of Miró's creative process. Franco was truly gone, and Spain breathed deep the oxygen of freedom, but too late for Roland to have given us an understanding of Miró's reaction to Fascist oppression in the first edition of this book.

As it was with Roland and Picasso, the strongest connective tissue between Roland and Miró became the surrealist poet Paul Eluard. In 1947 the Swiss publisher Gérald Cramer approached Miró with the idea to illustrate Eluard's book of poems *A Toute épreuve*, written nearly two decades earlier during the poet's break up with his wife Gala. Miró cut more

3

3 Joan Miró, Dominique (Odette Lemort) Eluard and Roland Penrose looking at work plate for *A Toute épreuve* by Paul Eluard, Atelier Lacourière-Frélaut, Paris, 1956 (photographed by Lee Miller)

than 230 woodblocks over a period of nearly eleven years to complete the 80 prints for this work.[5] He wrote to Cramer: 'I am completely absorbed by the damn book, I hope to create something sensational...'[6] Miró succeeded in making images with such vitality that they seemed to dance across the page.

Characteristically, Miró was not content with making a woodcut in its conventional form and relentlessly pushed the technical frontiers by building up the blocks like collages, incorporating pieces of rough wood plank, plastic, wire, old engravings and bark paper. Printing these highly diverse and sometimes fragile blocks required a genius of its own, in the form of Jacques Frélaut who, with his brother and sister, ran the famous printmaking workshop Atelier Lacourière-Frélaut in its original location near the Sacre Coeur.

In 1956, at the time of the printing, Roland was living in Paris with Lee Miller, while working for the British Council. With Miró and with Eluard's widow Dominique, they visited the Atelier Lacourière-Frélaut to see the work in progress. The collaboration would have given immense satisfaction to Eluard, but tragically his already fragile health had been fatally weakened during the war years when he and his second wife Nusch had, as a result of their activities publishing stridently anti-Nazi poems, been on the run from the Gestapo. Nusch died in 1946 and he followed in 1952. Just over a year before, he had married Dominique Laure. This meeting, then, was far

4 ABOVE Joan Miró, *Painting*, 1925
5 LEFT Joan Miró modifying *Painting*
1925, Farleys House, East Sussex,
1964 (photographed by Antony
Penrose)

more than an agreeable occasion where four old friends came together to see the progress of an exciting project. Eluard had been dearly loved by them all, and was no doubt firmly in their thoughts and their hearts in this instant, as they united in celebrating him and his work. Roland later wrote: 'The book that was the result of these labours is one of the most beautiful products of our century – a wonderful harmony between poet and painter.'[7]

Roland's 1960 Picasso retrospective for the Arts Council at the Tate Gallery (now Tate Britain) has been called 'the show of that century'. At the time it was recognized as being the first 'block buster', with a queue snaking around Millbank, and Roland was widely acknowledged for his curatorial skill and also his diplomacy in getting the loans. It was not surprising that the Picasso show was barely over before the Arts Council asked him to curate a major retrospective on Miró, again at the Tate.

Roland still had all the gallery plans and, as the loans were confirmed, he would make miniature mouse-sized paintings, placing them on the huge architect's drawings spread out on the dining room table in our home at Farley Farm in East Sussex. It was a protracted process, made more difficult by the cats jumping on the table and reorganizing the hang, but it gave a very clear organizational strategy so, when the time came to mount the show, it saved days of work.

Miró was due to come for the opening in August 1964, but he suffered a tragic bereavement when his son-in-law was killed in a car accident. It was in September, towards the end of the show, when he came and, although he loved seeing the faultless installation at the Tate, it was clear he did not want to do press and television interviews. Roland invited him and his wife Pilar, with their ceramicist collaborator Josep Artigas and his wife Violette, to Farleys. Also in the party were the photographer Joaquim Gomis and his wife Odette, long-time friends of Miró whose ebullience contrasted to Miró's calmness.

Miró loved the garden at Farleys. For long periods he would sit peacefully watching the trees and flowers. He seemed particularly to like the thrushes and blackbirds as they picked over the crumbly soil of the flower beds. He watched with kind but intense eyes, observing every detail. His stillness gave the impression of a meditating Buddhist monk, emanating his benign serenity for us to share.

Few of Miró's paintings remained in our house, as Roland had lent most of them to the Tate exhibition, but a large blue canvas titled *Painting* (1925) still hung in the sitting room. Miró studied it intently and then asked Roland if he could take it

4, 5

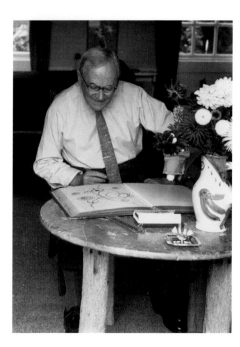

6 LEFT Joan Miró signing Farleys Visitors' Book, Farleys House, East Sussex, 14 September 1964 (photographed by Antony Penrose)
7 OPPOSITE Joan Miró, *Design for Desmond Morris*, 1964

down. He explained that seeing it after an interval of forty years made him want to bring it into the present, and asked for some paint. Roland found some old tubes of oil paint and a brush. They balanced the painting on an armchair and with deep fascination we watched Miró's long, silent contemplation. Would there be major changes? Would we still love the work as we did before? What colour would he choose?

He chose black. It was too dry, but the coarse short bristles allowed him to scrub the paint on to the surface. With great deliberation he gave the four, finely pointed forms semi-circular caps that took away their menace. Maybe he was concerned that they could hurt the vulnerable white creature as it swam in its aqueous environment.

The painting was returned to its hook on the wall, and first Artigas and then Miró settled down to sign our Farleys Visitors' Book. For me, Miró's design is a bird searching among the flowers of the herbaceous border. Under it he wrote:

Roland and Lee en souvenir de cet admirable séjour a la campagne et cet accueil si touchant, Miró, Pilar 19 – 9 – 64.

Roland and Lee in memory of this admirable stay in the country and the touching welcome, Miró, Pilar 19 – 9 – 64.

In 1950 Roland's London Gallery showed Miró's paintings in the main gallery beside two first one-man exhibitions of work by Cyril Hamersma and Desmond Morris. By 1964 Morris, still a surrealist painter but also a zoologist, had become Keeper of Mammals at London Zoo. On hearing of Miró's visit, he contacted Roland offering an invitation to go backstage at London Zoo. On Miró's enthusiastic acceptance, Morris asked which animals he would like to see. 'Large birds, snakes and creatures of the night,' came the reply.

The large bird was a hornbill that perched on Miró's wrist and gently took grapes from his fingers, tilting her head back so the grape rolled down inside her huge beak. The snake was a vast python draped around Miró's neck by Morris and one of the keepers. 'The creature of the night' Morris chose was a chameleon in a room lit so the animals thought it was night-time. This strange creature looked as if it had been designed by Miró himself. It sat motionless on a branch until Morris produced an insect stuck to the end of a small rod. In a flash a long tongue shot out and, with the soft 'clop' of its lips, the bug was gone.

In his office Morris produced a copy of an illustrated book of Miró's work. Would Miró please sign it? Of course, and Miró, still glowing from his encounter, drew a portrait of the chameleon.

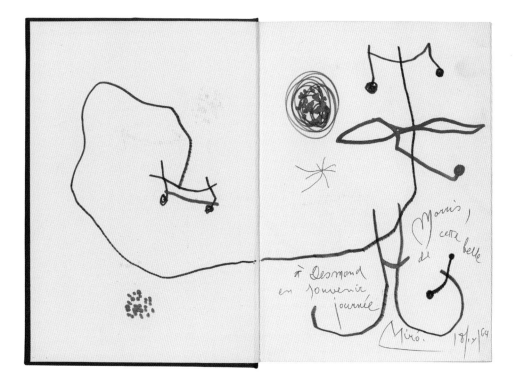

In the years that followed, Roland and Lee made several visits to Miró's studio in Majorca and to his farm in Montroig. There were fewer projects, but that gave more opportunity to enjoy the simple, earthy delights Miró surrounded himself with, although Roland was involved with the setting up of the Fundació Joan Miró in Barcelona where he, with a nice sense of reciprocity, had his own retrospective exhibition in 1981.[8]

Miró died on 25 December 1983. He was the last of Roland's key friends from his early life in France to leave the stage. Man Ray, Max Ernst, Picasso, Eluard, Duchamp, Valentine and Lee herself had all died by now, leaving him with a sense of loneliness and loss that could never be assuaged. These friendships were vital. They were forged against the looming threat of Fascism by a group who had experienced two world wars yet never lost their determination to champion the change of the world and our experience of it, even in the face of the bitter and sustained opposition of the establishment. The present-day level of esteem in which we hold them signals that THEY WON. Roland, if he allowed himself to, would feel proud of his role as their fellow artist, curator, biographer and friend.

Chapter 1
A Period of Growth

In an attempt to sum up the conflict which can take place in a poet or an artist between inspiration and reason, Guillaume Apollinaire described two different kinds of artist: those who accept without challenge the dictates of their muse, 'who are like a prolongation of nature and whose works in no way pass through the intelligence', and those others who 'must draw everything out of themselves and not at all from their daemonic urge, no muse inspires them. They live in solitude, and nothing is expressed except what they themselves utter in agitation.'[1]

It would be impossible to assign Joan Miró to either of these categories because he belongs essentially to both. To say that he was a 'prolongation of nature', guided subconsciously by his daemon, is a means of describing the highly personal qualities in his work which held him close to the marvels of nature all his life. At the same time he was by no means only an innocent poetic voice; there was in Miró a highly trained contemplative counterpart to unselfconscious spontaneity. He was also one of those artists whose expression comes, in Apollinaire's words, from 'effort upon effort, attempt after attempt, to formulate that which they desire to formulate'.[2]

It is probably necessary that all artists destined to achieve great eloquence should combine the mystery of inspiration with an intellect capable of probing not only the world around them but also the validity of their own work. This intellectual curiosity is necessary both for the extension and perfection of their own talent and for the mastery of techniques which can enlarge and enrich their means of expression. Miró was an artist who never lost his burning desire to experiment, and to probe deeper into the nature of reality, but intellect was never allowed to stifle imagination.

No artist had deeper roots in his homeland, and in the art of the past, than Miró. The artistic influences he absorbed from his contemporaries are diverse and often mysterious, but his inherited qualities are much more easily traced. By birth and by ancestry he was a Catalan, a native of the province of Catalonia which covers much of north-eastern Spain and includes the Balearic Islands. Although he travelled to many foreign countries, his native Catalonia had only one rival in his heart: France, where he had an active group of friends, and where the cultural atmosphere of Paris had attracted him for many years.

Joan Miró was born in Barcelona in 1893. He came of a line of skilled craftsmen. His father was a prosperous goldsmith who kept a shop in the Pasaje del Crédito, one of the narrow passages that still exist among the tightly packed blocks of houses and crowded streets in the heart of the old city. Close by on one side are the elegant arcades of the Plaza Real, leading into the Ramblas with their ceaseless flow of life, and on the other stand the ancient Gothic palaces that surround the Cathedral. But although he grew up amid the hubbub and the smells of a busy Mediterranean port, brilliant in its colours and the variety of its trade, Joan soon discovered that he was really more at home in the great open spaces of the Catalan countryside.

Early in life he announced to his family that he wished to become a painter, but his father turned a deaf ear. In 1910, at the age of seventeen, the young man found himself dutifully accepting a job as a clerk in an office. This made him so unhappy that in the following year he became seriously ill, and his father sent him to recover at a newly acquired farm near the foothills overlooking the coastal plain, south of Tarragona. This farm was to be a place of great importance in Miró's life. It consisted of a solidly built farmhouse surrounded by several acres of olive trees and vines. Near by was a hill town, called Montroig (red mountain) because of a shaggy outcrop of red rock neatly crowned by the masonry of a small chapel (a romantic feature which was to make its appearance in Miró's early landscapes). It was in this part of Catalonia that Miró's family had its roots: his paternal grandfather, whose name was also Joan Miró, had been a blacksmith in the ancient village of Cornudella de Montsant. As a child his grandson paid him frequent visits, not only for the sake of his rather fragile health but also because of the enchantment he found in the wild, rugged mountains and the fascination of the creatures, plants and flowers which became known to him in every detail.

The family of Dolores Ferrà, Joan's mother, came from Majorca. Her father was a cabinet-maker, which meant that Joan

8

8 *Cornudella. Hermitage of Sant Joan del Codolar,* undated

inherited from both sides of the family the traditions of skill
and style necessary for fine workmanship. It is, in consequence,
understandable that an inborn love of nature and the arts
should have led to a severe crisis due to a sense of frustration
when his father insisted on a business career. Before his
breakdown, Miró had occasionally managed to attend classes at
the Escuela de Bellas Artes, 'La Llotja', the same official academy
in Barcelona where, some twelve years before, Picasso had for
a brief moment astonished his professors with his prodigious
talent. Miró had been recognized by his tutors, Modesto Urgell
and José Pascó, as a promising pupil who could make pleasant
drawings from nature during his excursions to the mountain
villages; an early example of his inherited skill can be found in
a jewellery design. But he tells us with characteristic candour
that he gained there the reputation of being 'a phenomenon
of clumsiness'.

On his return from Montroig, once more in good health, Joan
was allowed to enter an art school in Barcelona which had as its
head a painter of great intelligence, Francisco Galí. This school
provided a very different atmosphere. Galí had devised ways of
awakening in his pupils an acute sense of observation. He took
them for excursions into the mountains, telling them to 'wear a
crown of eyes round their heads';[3] he encouraged them to take
an interest in chamber music and poetry. It was his teaching of

9 *Untitled (Snake),* design for jewellery, undated

drawing that impressed Miró most deeply. Placing an object in the hands of a blindfolded pupil, Galí told him to become so well acquainted with it by touch that he could afterwards draw what he had felt without seeing it. Under Galí's tuition Miró found that his perception of form and his ability to interpret it developed rapidly.

In 1915 he attended certain classes at the Sant Lluc circle, and met two other young artists, Joan Prats and Josep Llorens Artigas, with whom he formed lifelong friendships. The circle owed its reputation to a former student, the Art Nouveau architect Antoni Gaudí. His extraordinary inventions in building, which include the gigantic steeples of the cathedral of La Sagrada Família and the admirable decorations and terraces of the Parque Güell, had already stirred the enthusiasm of the younger generation in Barcelona. His use of flowing organic shapes, and his revolutionary techniques, influenced Miró deeply throughout his life.

In 1910 the rebellion against his father's plans for his future had coincided with Miró's dissatisfaction with the traditional methods of teaching art at La Llotja. This was the first

10 RIGHT *Untitled (Back of Nude)*, 1915
11 BELOW *Untitled (Market Scene)*, 1915

major crisis in a life which, since then, was punctuated with periodic upheavals, each bringing with it marked changes in Miró's work. Their frequency and violence were all the more remarkable because of his apparent calm and the gentleness of his nature. This inner fire was to break through again in 1919 when his discontent with the provincial atmosphere of Barcelona made him leave home to explore new horizons.

A consciousness of the great revolution that was taking place in the arts in Paris grew steadily in Miró. In 1916, an exhibition of French contemporary painting brought to Barcelona by the dealer Vollard had impressed him greatly, and when the Ballets Russes of Serge Diaghilev came in 1917–18 Miró eagerly watched the performances from the gallery. In 1917 he met the provocative and rebellious dadaist Francis Picabia, who between visits to New York exhibited some of his work in Barcelona and edited four numbers of his outrageous avant-garde magazine *391*, which contained his own drawings of machine-like constructions. Most of the text was written by him, but there were also contributions from Max Goth, Max Jacob and Georges Ribemont-Dessaignes, and a full-page *calligramme* by Apollinaire in which words and visual images were inextricably combined.

The infiltration of avant-garde ideas from Paris during the First World War gave Miró his first chance to appreciate the importance of the contemporary French poets. He became convinced that poetry and painting were inseparable, and felt an immediate sympathy for the poets Pierre Reverdy and Maurice Raynal, who also visited Barcelona. The attraction of Paris was strong, but as long as the war lasted Miró could not go there. Meanwhile, his growing restlessness was temporarily overcome by his concentration on his work. He began to paint in the small upstairs room at his home in the Pasaje del Crédito, the same room about which he was able to say, more than twenty years later, that he still painted in the room where he was born.

It became increasingly obvious that one day Miró would make his way to Paris, but before he left Barcelona he was already able to establish a reputation within a small circle. His friends Prats, Artigas and E. C. Ricart shared his ambitions and encouraged him. In 1918 he held his first one-man exhibition at the Galerías Dalmau. The paintings he showed astonished all who saw them, not so much by their subject-matter as by the brilliance of the colour and the originality of the style, already apparent even though he was at this time strongly influenced by the Fauve painters. Four types of subject had occupied his attention: still-life, landscape, portraits and nudes. The themes

12 *Still-life with Knife,* 1916

12

in themselves are ordinary enough, but there is something surprisingly new and personal in every picture. In the still-life studies of the familiar bottles, bowls, apples and flowers, each object has been seen with a new vision and examined for its own essential qualities. Each bottle or jar has a character of its own, its surface enclosing an intangible inner space. The apples are round and solid, spread on cloths which can sometimes be reminiscent of Cézanne, although painted with a brilliance of colour which belongs more to the daring experiments of the Fauves. Angular lines that thrust into the picture from the foreground create a convincing sense of the third dimension without the use of the conventional rules of perspective. In the landscapes, too, perspective is also completely lacking, and yet the eye seems to penetrate far into the distance. This may be caused by a path which leads in from a corner and twists into the picture with such vigour that it entices the eye deep into

13 *Siurana, the Path,* 1917

the landscape, where the spectator finds himself surrounded by trees and houses, with perhaps a church or a bridge, until he meets the sky, often filled with clouds shaped characteristically by the Mediterranean wind. Every detail has its rhythm, which is linked to the rhythms of the shapes around it, reminiscent of the arabesques and the bold calligraphy that we still find in Spanish peasant tradition, where every name painted on a cart has a compelling flourish so strong that the eye dances along with delight over each letter.

There is also a simplification of form that can be traced to cubist influences. Miró had seen the work of Picasso and Braque, chiefly in reproduction. He was attracted by cubism as a style though he did not share the same purpose of dissecting and analysing each object. He used angular forms to create a movement that led the eye deep into the picture. When the subject was a hill town such as Montroig, Miró interpreted the rectangular pattern of the houses, stacked closely together with cubist rigour like a hard geological formation. He had already abandoned the intention we find in his early drawings

of making a literal copy of the landscape and, wit
stems from the brilliant light of Catalonia, he cc
emotional appeal that his subject had made on
to make every part of the painting reveal its ov
meaning, whether it were a tree, a ploughed f
mountain, a house or the clouds, he no long
emphasize or deform its appearance according

Miró's treatment of reality came to a large degree
instinctive feeling for the rhythms which underlie the tradit
patterns of peasant art, and also from another equally strong
native tradition which is to be found in Romanesque Catalan
painting. Miró was thoroughly acquainted with the riches of
the early medieval frescoes that abounded in the churches of
Catalonia, each figure full of a characteristic life. Here, again,
there is the simplification of form, the flow of curves, and the
bold use of distortion to heighten the emotional effect, which
are typical of all Catalan art.

These influences show themselves strongly in some portraits
Miró made of his friends in Barcelona. In the portrait of the
painter Ricart (1917) he combines the influence of indigenous
Catalan culture with something of the expressionism of
Van Gogh. There is a freedom in his use of colour which is
reminiscent of the Fauves, but the violent rhythms of form
and colour, particularly in Ricart's striped jacket, are Miró's
own interpretation of the various styles that impressed him.
The portrait departs from the usual tendency to fill the
background with vigorous decorative elements which is to be
found in almost all Miró's still-life paintings of this period.
Here the figure is placed against a plain lemon-yellow wall on
which hangs the diagrammatic shape of the painter's palette,
but on the right the usual detail of patterned wallpaper or
curtains is replaced by a Japanese print stuck to the canvas,
a sign of Miró's continual search for new solutions.

Discussing the vigorous impact of this painting, Jacques
Dupin remarks: 'In front of the human figure Miró seems to be
seized by terror, overcome by giddiness to which he can only
respond by a violent reaction involving his own being.'[4] The
hieratic or even barbaric appearance of the figure, the strong
contrasts in colour and the abrupt transition in the background
suggest a disquiet on the part of the artist which can only be
overcome by a violence which borders on cruelty towards his
model, and this is even more apparent in the fierce dissection he
practises when he approaches the even more troubling presence
of the female nude. In the large painting *Standing Nude*, of 1918,
in which the figure is placed in front of patterns of brilliantly
coloured materials, Miró's deliberate analysis of the female form

14

15

14 ABOVE *Portrait of Enric Cristòfol Ricart*, 1917
15 OPPOSITE *Standing Nude*, 1918

16 ABOVE *Nude
with Mirror,* 1919
17 RIGHT *Portrait of a
Young Girl,* 1919

is neither flattering nor tender. The figure is built solidly, with the determination of an artist who will not allow one grain of sentimentality to weaken his work, who is so deeply moved by his subject that it is only by the clearest, most uncompromising statement that he is able to express his reaction.

16
17 The same objective candour appears again in the *Nude with Mirror* of 1919, but here, as in the *Portrait of a Young Girl* of the same year, Miró with admirably controlled precision allows a lyrical tenderness, such as is rare in his work, to illuminate the painting.

The realistic appeal of these early versions, when compared with the later evolution of Miró's image of women, is of great interest. As Dupin suggests, there is usually a feeling of disquiet. This may be considered as a tribute to the mysterious problem of the representation of the human form, and in particular to the power of female magic. Miró's early purpose was a bold analysis of form, which later became an interpretation or a symbol of the meaning of the female presence as an integral part of the human condition. This could best be understood by paradox and by signs. It is the universal and magical influence of women that has preoccupied him continuously, rather than the more obvious charms of the female form. We shall see later the violence and significance of his reactions to it.

The originality and strength of Miró's work when it was shown at the Galerías Dalmau in 1918 was sufficient to convince his friends, and a small number of the more sensitive people who saw it, that a young painter of outstanding ability had appeared among them; but to the public in general his paintings were incomprehensible. This apathy convinced him that Barcelona was not the climate in which he could develop, and in 1919 he left at last for Paris.

This first contact with Paris was not wholly successful, although from then on he returned every winter. It was inevitable that those whose company he enjoyed should be as impoverished as himself; and, since the sale of his paintings was even more hazardous in a foreign city than at home, his only consolations for living on the verge of starvation were the museums and the excitement of contacts with friends who did understand and appreciate his work. Among them was
18 Picasso, who bought from the young Catalan a self-portrait, recently finished after long concentration on the precision and stylization of every detail. This painting, remarkable for the strength of its honest naïveté, was a development of an earlier, less successful, self-portrait showing Fauve influences. It remained one of Picasso's most treasured possessions.

18 ABOVE *Self-portrait*, 1919
19 OPPOSITE *The Vegetable Garden with Donkey*, 1918

The Seduction of Nature

As often happens when an artist is confronted with his work assembled in unfamiliar surroundings, dramatic changes came about in Miró's style after the 1918 Dalmau exhibition. Before that first visit to Paris in 1919, he had already become fascinated by well-defined detail, which could be situated in a painting so that it concentrated interest on certain areas and contributed to the rhythmic overall distribution of form. His former somewhat clumsy brushwork with its Fauve influences gave way to clearly defined outline, and a new stylization of form showed more clearly than before the precise rhythmical influence of traditional Catalan art.

It was in 1919, during the long summer days back at Montroig, that Miró developed his new style. He was able there to contemplate in detail the rhythms of growth in plants or trees around him, and on a larger scale, the patterns of the cultivated fields and the outline of the distant mountains. Paintings such as *Mont-roig, Vineyards and Olive Trees* and *Montroig, Church and*

20 ABOVE *Mont-roig, Vineyards and Olive Trees*, 1919
21 OPPOSITE *Horse, Pipe and Red Flower*, 1920

Village, both painted in 1919, have the quality of richly decorated embroidery, with the additional sense of deep recession into the distance, and a relation to reality which is in no way achieved by atmospheric effects or by the conventional rules of perspective.

There are still-life paintings belonging to this period, such as *Horse, Pipe and Red Flower* (1920), which were painted among the objects and furniture of the farmhouse itself. We find in these that the florid exuberance of his earlier brushwork and colour has come under a strict control. The Fauve influence has given way to that of cubism, but without any slavish surrender on the artist's part. The disruption of form, and the severe, penetrating analysis, typical of early cubism, are absent. Each object is examined and treated individually in a representational style. Distortion is used only to strengthen the composition, which is held together in clearly defined geometric structure. Only the use of localized colour, and the deliberate lack of three-dimensional depth, relate these paintings to cubist techniques. To avoid a complete sensation of enclosure, however, Miró cleverly brings the distant landscape into the still-life as a reflection in the mirror.

We find the same approach in another still-life of 1920 known as *The Table*, in which he has greatly elaborated the presentation of familiar objects without imparing the homogeneity of his statement. The curves of the table legs lead vigorously upwards to a square top set with a rich feast for the eye; a rabbit and a cock give an undoubted impression of life, as do some vine leaves and vegetables. In contrast, there are a tattered dead fish and a heavy earthenware jar. All these are held in the grip of the bold angular patterns of the table-top and napkin, which recall the rugged peaks of the distant horizon. Miró has succeeded in capturing here an extension of realism that carries us beyond the exact representation of each object, and beyond the rigid stylization with which they are painted. The still-life breaks out into the life of the open air. The limited space, the furniture and the well-known farmhouse objects become a window to a wide field of associations and distant visual echoes.

These paintings reveal a development towards the creation of a personal style in which Miró could follow his desire to extend his sense of reality and indulge his great ability to use precise and exquisite detail. They culminate in a large canvas,

22 *The Table (Still-life with Rabbit)*, 1920

23 *The Farm, 1921–22*

23   *The Farm* (1921–22). This early masterpiece is a truthful account
of the farmyard at Montroig, which he had known intimately
for ten years. It is a sign of Miró's deep attachment to his early
surroundings that he owned this property throughout his life
and returned there frequently to work. His familiarity with
every detail and his love of the quiet rhythm of the life of this
classical Mediterranean countryside made the task of painting
this picture one of prolonged devotion. The canvas travelled
with him when he left Montroig at the end of the summer of
1921; he continued it in Barcelona and completed it in his
studio in Paris, where he had brought samples of grasses
from Montroig.

    The scene gives an accurate description of the many
activities of a Catalan farmyard. It includes a woman washing

clothes, a horse raising water from the well, a dog barking, birds, animals, insects, snails, lizards and even the cracks in the plastered walls. The character of every object, from building to stone and blades of grass, is captured with great care; each exists both independently and as an element essential to the whole composition. To convey so much information in one picture without confusion or overcrowding is in itself a triumph. It could only be achieved by a masterly restraint, a sense of design and an understanding of the way in which rhythms, harmonies and echoes can be made to work together to form a homogeneous composition. There is a ruthless elimination of irrelevant detail which makes it possible for Miró to establish poetic associations or 'rhymes' between unrelated objects, giving new significance to each. These links occur because of resemblances made easily recognizable by the clear definition of the shapes. For instance, the sun which shines in a clear blue sky is not required to cast shadows; instead it is linked to the earth in another way. The circle representing its presence is made to contrast with a round black hole in the earth from which grows the central feature of the picture, a giant eucalyptus tree. The circle again finds an echo in the round red and blue hole in the water trough on which a cock is standing. This is in turn balanced on the left of the picture by the red wheel of the cart. These deliberate repetitions or reversals of form or colour joined by intermediary rhythmic patterns create by cross-reference a visual and conceptual unity within the composition. They provoke unlimited speculation on the endless play there can be between contrast and similarity, between negative and positive.

Since the painting is to some extent an inventory of those things and creatures that had interested Miró most deeply for many different reasons, it is not surprising that they should become the prototypes of symbols that recur throughout his later work. For instance, the ladder with a bird perching on it later develops into one of his obsessive signs, the ladder of escape, which provides a means of communication between the tangible and the intangible. Here it rises from the solid earth to become a perch where birds can find safety or fly away. The ladder is also related by its shape to a stool near the centre of the picture which stands out clearly like a large capital A, reminding us of the frequent and significant use that Miró makes of letters and numbers throughout his work.

24 Another painting of major importance, *Interior (The Farmer's Wife)* (1922–23), was begun in Montroig and finished in Paris. While still closely linked in sentiment with *The Farm*, it introduces some startling new developments.

24 *Interior (The Farmer's Wife)*, 1922–23

There is stringent simplification of form and deliberate distortion. The extraordinary disproportion between the woman's feet and the other parts of her anatomy is new and prophetic. There is also a surprising contrast between the style of the amiable but monstrous cat, which, like the rabbit and the woman, is candidly representational, and the schematic drawing of the charcoal fire and the chimney behind it. The hearth is indicated by a pale circle in the foreground above which a line mounts like a step with sharp angular bends towards the profile of a large black cowl, its chimney. There is a new freedom, a fantasy, and a disregard for homogeneity of both style and scale, which herald further revolutions in Miró's work but which do not destroy the overall harmony of the composition.

The gigantic feet of the farmer's wife, however, have a more personal significance. To quote Jacques Dupin: 'It may seem strange that the expression of the fantastic should break into the work of Miró through the feet of the farmer's wife. But as Miró has said on many occasions, it is by the feet, and from the earth, that the energy that transfigures reality mounts.'[5] In his desire to penetrate to the essence of reality, Miró found that contact with the earth and its magnetism is a factor as important as perception through the other senses. It is simple, banal and yet at the roots of our understanding. He knew throughout out that it is from terra firma, the sun-bleached soil, with its appetizing scent of plants, its dust, mud and weatherworn rocks, that we enter and enjoy the great open spaces, the all-invading light of day and the coolness of the stars by night. Just as the permanent foundation of the ground provides the springboard for voyages into outer space, so it is with the more mysterious flights of the imagination.

Chapter 2
Paris and Surrealism

From 1920 onwards, Miró worked during his winter visits to Paris in a studio in the rue Blomet which had been found for him by Llorens Artigas. In 1921, a small exhibition was staged at the Galerie La Licorne, with canvases from the Galerías Dalmau. This exhibition had the distinction of a preface by Maurice Raynal, but even so it was a complete failure.

It was in the rue Blomet, in 1922, that Miró made the acquaintance of André Masson, whose studio was separated from his only by a partition. Masson was to leave a lasting impression:

Masson was always a great reader and full of ideas. Among his friends were practically all the young poets of the day. Through Masson I met them – through them I heard poetry discussed. The poets Masson introduced me to interested me more than the painters I had met in Paris. I was carried away by the new ideas they brought and especially the poetry they discussed. I gorged myself on it all night long – poetry principally in the tradition of Jarry's Surmâle....[1]

Masson was closely involved with a group of young revolutionaries. Their ideas, which were concerned with the arts and politics in the widest sense, led them inevitably to unite with André Breton, Paul Eluard and Louis Aragon who were at that time bringing surrealism into existence; Breton recorded later that 'the tumultuous entrance of Miró in 1924 marks an important point in the development of surrealist art'.[2] Although the word 'tumultuous' would seem inappropriate when applied to an artist who was always known to his friends as shy, reserved and taciturn, we can gather from its use here the impression made on the French poet by this young Catalan, illuminated by the fire that sprang from the inner forces of his imagination and producing work that was strangely original and disturbing in its power.

The revolutionary activity which was astir among this group of young poets and artists who had lived through the misery and disillusionment of the First World War had coincided with a deep conviction in Miró that there was an urgent necessity to discover new methods and new ways of life. The dadaists, with whom he had come into contact both in Barcelona and in Paris, had thrown their insults at the conventional conceptions of art that belonged to a social system which had confirmed its hidebound inadequacy, but their destructive ardour eventually became tedious for those who wished to penetrate deeper into the fundamental nature of inspiration and the arts. The result was surrealism.

Among his new friends, those with whom Miró found himself particularly in sympathy were Michel Leiris, a scholarly, introspective poet and anthropologist with a love and understanding of primitive rites and exotic forms of art; Robert Desnos, poet and ardent explorer of the dangerous labyrinths of hallucination and hysteria; and the disconcertingly brilliant actor Antonin Artaud, who declaimed his hatred of organized religion in exultant prose and called for a determined blow for the liberation of the spirit. 'Abandon the caverns of existence. Come, the spirit breathes outside the spirit. It is time to leave home. Surrender to Universal Thought. The Marvellous is at the root of the spirit.'[3]

Before this outburst the new attitude had been more clearly formulated by André Breton in the first *Manifeste du surréalisme*, published in 1924. In spite of violent arguments the surrealists had arrived at an agreement that art is valid only when it has an equivalence with reality. They claimed that since all attempts at a logical analysis of reality had failed, the approach to a deeper understanding of consciousness should be, as Freud had already stated, through the subconscious.

The turbulence that emanated from the activities of the surrealists during these early days was to the outside world its most obvious characteristic. But in addition to their determination to assert the capital importance of art in human society, Miró greatly appreciated their insistence on creating a fusion between poetic and visual imagery, and their belief that every effort must be made to widen the scope of our perception. With this in view, it became necessary to explore by every possible means the unfathomed realms of the subconscious. Dreams, hallucinations, even hysteria and madness were the obvious paths that must be followed in order to penetrate unhindered beyond the recognized frontiers.

25 *The Ploughed Field*, 1923–24

Some years later, Miró explained to the artist and writer Yvon Taillandier how these views had affected him. 'I liked surrealism', he said, 'because the surrealists didn't consider painting as an end. With painting, in fact, we shouldn't care whether it remains such as it is, but rather whether it sets the germs of growth, whether it sows seeds from which other things will spring.'[4]

The subversive impact on Miró of these ideas, in combination with his natural tendency towards searching self-criticism, began at once to be seen in his work. A painting that he

25 produced in the winter of 1923–24 called *The Ploughed Field* might have been expected to be the direct sequel to *The Farm*, but we find in it a very different approach to reality. Here the world of the imagination has become supreme. He presents us with a phantasmagoria in which ears and eyes grow on trees and the beasts of the field take on new and disproportionate shapes. Miró explained later that he had managed to escape into 'the absolute of nature', and that his landscapes have 'nothing to do with external reality'. 'They are nevertheless', he said, 'more essentially Montroig than if they had been painted from nature.'

Paris and Surrealism

From this time onwards, the mainspring of Miró's vision comes from a new source. It is by the eye of the imagination that he is guided, and it provides him with an inexhaustible abundance of images. His confidence in this new approach was strengthened by the surrealists' belief that the visions of the imagination must be counted as part of reality. Their argument was that used by William Blake, that 'what is now proved was once only imagined'.

Between 1922 and 1925 Miró's work continued to develop with a wealth of invention in form, and with the same exquisite attention to detail. The knowledge he had gained from his study of insects, fish, birds and all the extravagant invention of nature, was translated into paintings such as *Carnival of Harlequin* and *Dialogue of Insects*, both of 1924–25. These pictures become a riotous playground in which the size and shape of each object or creature are adapted to give it the precise movement and the characteristic expression Miró desires. But with his childlike enjoyment of disproportionate limbs and features, and his entirely personal sense of which colours are appropriate, Miró exercises a decisive control, with the result that his extravaganzas become a miraculously well-ordered dance. Concealed in their movement, we find

26, 27

26 BELOW *Carnival of Harlequin*, 1924–25
27 OPPOSITE *Dialogue of Insects*, 1924–25

a strict rhythm which unifies form and colour throughout the canvas.

But the process which gave birth to these works was extremely arduous. 'For *Carnival of Harlequin* I made many drawings', he tells us, 'in which I expressed my hallucinations brought on by hunger. I came home at night without having dined and noted my sensations on paper. That year I often frequented poets because I felt I must get beyond *la chose plastique* [three-dimensional objects] to reach poetry.'[5]

It was probably the capricious fantasy of paintings such as *Carnival of Harlequin* that earned for Miró the reputation of being frivolous and even childish. 'Gaiety, sunshine, health – colour, humour, rhythm: these are the notes that characterize the work of Joan Miró' was to be the opening statement in James Johnson Sweeney's catalogue for the first important Miró exhibition in New York in 1941.[6] Although a childlike fantasy, an innocent sense of humour and an eager enjoyment of the grotesque have never abandoned him, there is even in these early works a poetic power, a precision and an intensity in colour, form and every detail which

28 *The Hunter (Catalan Landscape)*, 1923–24

remove them from the naïve and the trivial. They carry us beyond our first interpretations of their meaning into associations and analogies which can evoke unprecedented and significant discoveries.

28   Another of the paintings of the early 1920s, *The Hunter (Catalan Landscape)*, of 1923–24, is an example of the inventiveness of Miró's pictorial language and the originality of his sense of humour. Some of its cryptic signs are delightfully understandable, others keep their secret. The thought which has resulted in a particular fantastic shape is sometimes relatively easy to trace. For instance, we recognize the bearded head of the hunter from his bristling moustache, his keen eye, his large attentive ear and the delicate curve of his pipe, although the shapes and the placings of these features are unnaturalistic. In the same language of signs we are given the clue to his body and legs, which are indicated by angular lines, and the curve of his arms, in which he holds on one side a dead bird and on the other a long conical shape which we recognize from the flame it emits as his gun. In the foreground is his quarry. The shape of its head and ear suggests a rabbit, but its body is reduced to a long straight line encircled by dotted lines and finishing in a triangular fish-like tail. There are other attributes to this ambiguous creature, shapes which evoke in a kind of visual shorthand the internal organs, just as the heart of the hunter all aflame is also clearly visible; the long flourish

of a tongue reaches out from the rabbit's head towards a winged insect. These fragmentary signs are accompanied by the first four letters of the name of the traditional Catalan folk-dance, the *sardana*, splendidly inscribed in the foreground. This all adds up in simple terms to a poem inspired by the bucolic pleasures of a Catalan peasant who lives between a sunlit winter sky and a warm rose-coloured soil.

The Hunter is an example of Miró's ability to invent his own language of signs. During this early period the interpretation of the symbols can often be literal; each factor acts its part in the scene, united with the others by bonds which are often implied rather than made visible. The whole composition is held together by the unity of the background and the visual rhythm set up by the signs themselves as they lead the eye from one point to another.

In the *Portrait of Madame K* (1924) Miró dismembers the female form in the same way as he dislocates both the hunter and his prey. With a deliberate disregard for objective appearances and scale, he selects details which emphasize

29 *Portrait of Madame K*, 1924

the presence of a woman. The picture is in monochrome; a mixture of oil and bold lines in charcoal makes a strong contrast with the pale, unadorned background. It is easy to recognize the basic elements of the female form: head, breasts, heart and the spinal column which finishes in an inverted arrowhead decorated with flame-like wisps of pubic hair. But in addition there are other signs which remain enigmatic, and which again provide a dream-like atmosphere in which the imagination is given its freedom. There is here a provocative gap between the precise delineation of Miró's signs and our interpretations, but if we accept that there is no need for a literal translation, and recognize that he is speaking in terms of subconscious visual sensations which have their own indecipherable reality, we can then enjoy them just as we enjoy the inexplicable construction of a flower.

The language invented by Miró in this painting creates a symbol which, I would claim, has a validity parallel to that of the word 'woman'. Indeed, it evokes an image of even more universal significance, since the understanding of a word is limited to those who speak one language. The word 'woman' is a sign which has great prestige, and with which we are very familiar, but it is after all no more than a sequence of sounds or letters which separately have no apparent analogy with the idea of woman and which to an Inuit mean nothing. Miró creates an aspect of reality in visual form, in which each syllable has an

30 BELOW *The Family*, 1924
31 OPPOSITE *Maternity*, 1924

authenticity comparable to that of the word, but richer,
and eventually more widely understood.

30   In *The Family*, painted in the same year, and also in
monochrome, some of the same symbols are used in a
composition which is complicated by the presence of three
figures, father, mother and son. A third painting of singular
31   importance, *Maternity* (1924), is also closely linked with the
Portrait of Madame K and *The Family*. There is an obvious
similarity in the woman's head, which is represented by a simple
black shape crowned with hair radiating from it, but otherwise
the symbols clearly defined on a pale blue background have
become more cryptic. The body of the mother is condensed
into a black conical shape pierced by a round hole. It appears

32 *Head of a Catalan Peasant*, 1925

to swing like a pendulum hung by a thin straight line from the head, while two small embryonic creatures, potentially human, climb towards shapes which we recognize as the woman's breasts. One breast is seen in profile and the other as a circle which could also be an eye or even the sun. Between them a shape – fish or spermatozoon – swims through the all-enveloping ether. There is an obvious resemblance between these small eager creatures and parasites that cling like children for food and protection to a parent body. The artist and writer Marcel Jean points out that 'many of Miró's paintings appear indeed to be portraits, sometimes burlesque, but more often menacing, of parasitic insects considerably enlarged'. In *Maternity* 'the movement towards the breasts is still tentative, but we feel the force of attraction; elsewhere we shall find that Miró uses this fundamental force, this suction, to imply tension. The oral attachment of rudimentary organic forms is to be found frequently creating a sensation which is both attractive and repulsive to us but inevitably compulsive.'[7]

This picture is of interest because it demonstrates a further development in Miró's use of symbols. Renouncing the diversity of images and detail with which he had enjoyed enriching earlier paintings, here he uses signs with strict economy and places them in a significant relation to each other. They are so linked and move so inevitably together that they have an organic unity, becoming a single anatomy that floats in a clear luminous element. This complex taken as a whole produces a new visual image of maternity which evokes in us deep reactions and a wealth of associations. It brings with it the conviction that we are approaching a new or perhaps very primitive sense of reality.

A New Vision of Reality: 'Dream Paintings'
In 1923 Miró had exhibited in the conventional atmosphere of the Salon d'Automne with some other Catalan painters. In the same year he made the acquaintance of Ernest Hemingway, Jacques Prévert and Henry Miller. Hemingway later became the owner of *The Farm*, a painting which he declared years later he would exchange for no other in the world. This sale, brought about largely through the efforts of Miró's friend Jacques Viot, was the beginning of a much-needed relief from the poverty in which Miró had been living, and for the next few years a modest prosperity slowly came his way.

Miró also found in Pierre Loeb a dealer who was convinced of his talent, and in 1925 an exhibition at the Galerie Pierre brought the first considerable success, although it was founded largely on curiosity and scandal, a contribution to this being

33 *Painting-Poem (Photo: This Is the Colour of My Dreams)*, 1925

the preface to the catalogue by the surrealist Benjamin Péret. Over the next few years, a continuous showing of surrealist painters selected by Pierre Loeb gave Miró the opportunity to exhibit his 'dream paintings' in this gallery. In March 1926 the new Galerie Surréaliste advertised Miró as one of its artists in a list which included André Masson, Yves Tanguy, Giorgio de Chirico, Man Ray, Rrose Sélavy (Marcel Duchamp), Francis Picabia, Georges Malkine, Pablo Picasso and Max Ernst. In these two neighbouring galleries the most recent paintings of Miró were always on view.

The path that Miró had taken, which led him to draw increasingly on the subconscious, was bringing about a new crisis. A reaction against the pictures composed of isolated details encouraged him to banish such complications from his painting in favour of a more simple statement. The change is perhaps most strikingly expressed in a picture of 1925 which consists simply of an oval shape painted in blue on the bare white canvas. Crossing it in bold calligraphy are the words

33   *Photo/ceci est la couleur de mes rêves*; 'This is the colour of my dreams.'

By the winter of 1924–25 Miró, while absorbing many surrealist ideas, had begun to assert a very personal influence among the surrealists. After the culmination of his early work, in *The Farm*, he had developed a new lyrical freedom, but with characteristic rigour he demanded of himself a clarification of

31   purpose which can already be seen in *Maternity* and which he proceeded to carry further, urged on by the surrealist appeal to explore the depths of the subconscious.

At an early age Miró had understood the necessity for a continuous questioning of his own achievements. He once said: 'Above all, never let a holy disquiet be lacking', and he tells us, too: 'When I was not content with my work I banged my head against the wall.' A study of his sudden changes of style and the challenges he set himself will convince us that the apparent tranquillity with which he worked was the surface tension necessary to contain the enthusiasms and agonies that were continuously at work in the depths of his thought.

The surrealists had helped to stimulate his ideas and suggest new methods of externalizing the riches of his inspiration. In their view it was important to explore not only the subconscious but also chance. The surprises which chance happenings could contribute to works of the imagination had been demonstrated first by Marcel Duchamp, and soon after by Max Ernst. It can be said that, since these early discoveries, chance has gained the reputation of one of the great impresarios of our time. Even so, it is the ability of the artist to recognize the peculiar virtues of the gifts they receive by chance that allows those virtues to become significant. Paradoxically, with increasing skill and the assurance of a magician, Miró gained a mastery over the uncontrollable, and he worked in harmony with the unpredictable. Achievements such as these, which came naturally to him, won for him Breton's statement: 'He may be considered the most surrealist among us.'[8]

The subconscious, which acts from within, and which is subjective just as chance is objective, was examined with great enthusiasm by the surrealists. Encouraged by the doctrines of Freud, they made extensive experiments in automatism, deliberately suspending conscious control in order to release an unhindered flow of subconscious thought. Among the poets who made the most thorough research into the sources of inspiration, encouraging states of hallucination and risking madness, were Miró's friends – Robert Desnos and Antonin Artaud.

In his search for a new visual language Miró entered willingly, as in paintings such as *Head of a Pipe-smoker* (1925), into the conscious attempts of the surrealists to liberate the subconscious; but his independent, taciturn character helped him to realize that such activities could only be a more or less successful means to an end which could be sensed rather than defined: the liberation of the spirit.

Ever since his arrival in Paris Miró had soaked himself in the works of the French poets, Rimbaud, Lautréamont, Jarry, Apollinaire, the precursors of surrealist ideas:

As a result of this reading I began gradually to work away from the realism I had practised up to The Farm, *until in 1925 I was drawing almost entirely from hallucinations. At the time I was living on a few dried figs a day. I was too proud to ask my colleagues for help. Hunger was a great source of these hallucinations. I would sit for long periods looking at the bare walls of my studio trying to capture* *these shapes on paper or burlap.*[9]

34 LEFT *Head of a Pipe-smoker*, 1925
35 OPPOSITE *Painting*, 1925

The canvases that now followed have been called 'dream paintings', not because Miró was painting from memory what he had dreamed, but rather because they had their origin to a large degree in the subconscious and were executed with the greatest possible spontaneity. This approach corresponded to the experiments of the surrealists in automatic writing and the random choice of pictorial images; but Miró's originality was sufficiently strong to make his 'dream paintings' a new and revolutionary form of expression. This happened chiefly because of his ability to eliminate elaborations and additions introduced by conscious control; suppressing even the symbols that were later to reappear with new significance, he arrived occasionally at pictures which, stripped of all irrelevances, relied on a small spot of colour against an atmospheric background to give a sensation of infinite depth. This kind of abstraction, which gives a sense of space without the aid of geometry, created the elemental conditions in which Miró could situate forms that floated freely or were held in a state of tension in relation to each other.

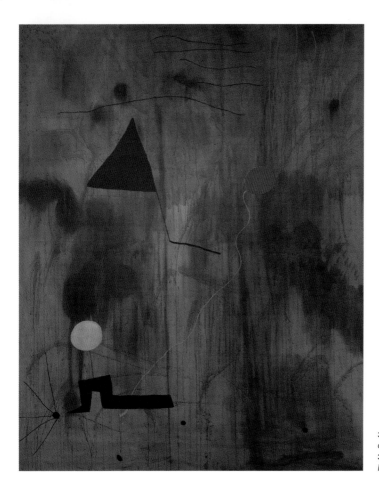

36 LEFT *The Birth of the World*, 1925
37 OPPOSITE *The Policeman*, 1925

36 Even in those works most thoroughly stripped of recognizable signs, such as *The Birth of the World* (1925), we realize that the things we see are not vague abstractions. These paintings convey the impression of a mysterious cosmic event. Apparently incompatible bodies float in an ether, liquid or gaseous. They seem to be drawn together in spite of themselves, and their inevitable meeting seems to signify some imminent disaster or revelation. Yet all this happens without pretension. The forms are rudimentary and their colours unadulterated; often they are reduced to the simplicity of white or black. But it is the background, alive with the subtleties of chance happenings and creating an all-enveloping atmospheric distance, which sets the stage for dream-like encounters, striking up a compulsive dance among forms so incongruous that nothing but forces beyond

their control could attract them towards each other. But, again, Miró never allowed his sense of humour and his delight in the absurd to leave him, as may be seen in works such as *Lovers* and *The Policeman*, of 1925, and numerous drawings of the same period. Once more his conviction that he must keep his feet on the ground in order to reach transcendental heights saved him from vacant forms of abstraction.

In the 'dream paintings' of 1925–26 there is great restraint in colour and an elimination of the overcrowded descriptive details of earlier years. Instead we find, in general, linear signs reminiscent of the graffiti by which vagrants make known their clandestine movements. These are combined

38 ABOVE *Painting-Poem (Le corps de ma brune puisque je l'aime comme ma chate habillée en vert salade comme de la grêle c'est pareil)*, 1925
39 OPPOSITE *Painting-Poem (Un oiseau poursuit une abeille et la baisse)*, 1927

with clearly defined flat shapes, spectral forms which in spite of their lack of representational qualities somehow obtain a life of their own. Their signification is often ambiguous. Some of them have biomorphic references, whereas others are so far abstracted from their origins that we relate them more easily to the mysterious images that appear in states of semi-consciousness. At other times Miró intensified the enigmatic poetic significance of his paintings by the startling appearance of a number, a word or a phrase. Developing a technique which owed much to Apollinaire's *calligrammes*, and which had been used more recently by Max Ernst, Miró produced poem-paintings such as the large canvas with a rich brown background, *Le corps de ma brune...* of 1925, on which he wrote in powerful calligraphy across symbols of breasts and hair: *le corps de ma brune/puisque je l'aime/comme ma chatte habillée en vert salade/comme de la grêle/c'est pareil* ('my brown girl's body/ since I love her/like my she-cat dressed in salad-green/like hail/ it's the same'). In the 1927 painting *Un oiseau poursuit une abeille et la baisse* [*sic*] ('A bird pursues a bee and lowers [ravishes] it'), the word *poursuit* is given the eccentric course of the bird's flight; in *Amour* (1926), a large shape like a head is embraced by the letters of the word *amour* (love) starting from a small round

38

39

40

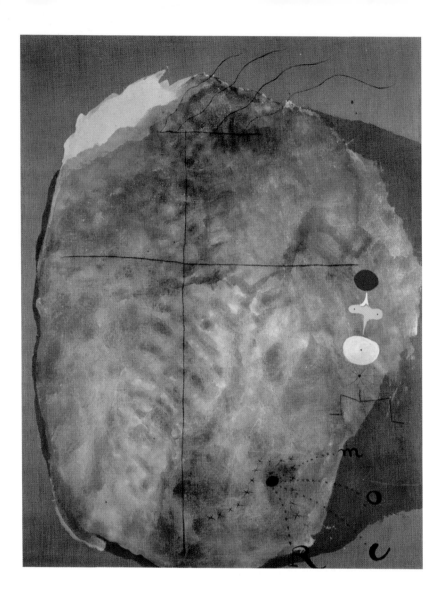

40 ABOVE *Painting-Poem (Amour),* 1926
41 OPPOSITE *Painting-Poem (Le signe de la mort),* 1927

mouth and finishing with two small anthropomorphic signs, the male climbing upwards in pursuit of the female.

His messages are not always light-hearted. Miró has the ability to strike a note of terror with the most elementary means, as in the small painting of 1927 where, on a patch of bright red with the plain canvas as its background, he has written *Le signe de la mort*, 'The sign of death', an announcement made strangely dramatic by its link with the white circle above it which is crossed out with two thin lines and inscribed with the number 133. There is no monotonous formula; in other paintings such as *Dog Barking at the Moon* and *Person Throwing a Stone at a Bird*, both of 1926, no letters or numbers are used. The forms are closer to the more representational figures of earlier work, with brilliant touches of colour like small flames breaking out at vulnerable points. There is no longer any definable difference between the representation and the symbol.

41

42

43

42 ABOVE *Dog Barking at the Moon,* 1926
43 OPPOSITE *Person Throwing a Stone at a Bird,* 1926

The Rue Tourlaque

In 1927 Miró left his friends in the rue Blomet to move into a studio that had been offered him by his dealer Jacques Viot, in the Cité des Fusains in Montmartre, on the rue Tourlaque. On the door he put up a sign he had found in a shop saying TRAIN PASSANT SANS ARRÊT, 'Non-stop train passing'. In this back street bordering on a cemetery he again found himself surrounded by a colony of surrealists who lived in adjoining studios. His neighbours were Max Ernst, René Magritte, Jean Arp and that sensitive creator of enthusiasm, the poet Paul Eluard, who gained Miró's lasting friendship by the warmth of his nature and the clarity of his thought.

Among the painters it was Arp who, in the detachment of his character and in the style he had evolved, resembled Miró most closely. As early as 1916 Arp had produced coloured wood reliefs. The shapes he used were 'biomorphic' abstractions of natural or commonplace objects in simple flowing curves, impregnated with an astringent sense of humour. There is a close parallel between them and the 'dream paintings' of Miró. We know how they enjoyed each other's company, and even the poverty they shared, 'eating radishes and butter', and it has been suggested that Miró was strongly influenced by Arp. However, Marguerite Hagenbach, Arp's second wife, told the art historian Sam Hunter in 1958 that 'Arp would say that you cannot really speak of influence, though, of course, Miró was impressed by certain signs and symbols of Arp and perhaps used some of them in his personal way.'[10]

Although there is a similarity between the shapes we find in the work of both artists, there is an important difference in their approach. Whether using his favourite technique of making configurations and arrangements formed by chance, or employing more deliberate methods, Arp was searching for a new aesthetic of form. His 'inarticulate form-experiences', of which Herbert Read speaks in his book on the artist, become 'none the less significant at an unconscious level of the psyche',[11] whereas Miró's forms have a more directly symbolic value. Arp was therefore justified in affirming that 'the signs of Miró are closer to those of Catalan folklore and children's symbols'.[12]

Apart from stylistic affinities, Miró also was impressed by the earlier activities of Arp. In Zurich during the war Arp had been, with Tristan Tzara, one of the most brilliant and provocative initiators of Dada, and had followed this up by collaborating with Max Ernst in Cologne in 1920, when the scandalous Dada exhibition they organized was closed down on the orders of the occupying British authorities. Despite his reputation as a revolutionary, however, Arp disclosed the underlying serenity and seriousness of his character when he wrote years later: 'We were seeking an art based on fundamentals, to cure the madness of the age, and a new order of things that would restore the balance between heaven and hell.'[13]

Max Ernst had been a close friend of Arp for many years, having shared with him the rebellious scorn of the dadaists before tempering his bitterness in the more creative spirit of surrealism. There was in Ernst, however, a malefic humour which estranged him from Miró. The underlying rivalry between them was accompanied by a keen interest in each other's work. Living at such close quarters, the shy withdrawal of Miró and the more extravert vitality of Ernst resulted in a long-remembered event which could have ended in disaster. Ernst, with his usual generosity, had shown Miró all his most recent work, including the new methods of collage and frottage which were then his latest inventions, but Miró was reticent. He told Ernst that he had been warned by his dealer that no one must see his paintings before his next exhibition. Ernst's annoyance came to a head one evening when he had some surrealist friends with him in his studio. The lights fused, and, reduced to three candles, they sat drinking and watching Miró, whose lighting was unaffected, continuing to paint on the floor below. After a while, enticed by the light, Ernst and his friends made a surprise descent on Miró, who welcomed them and added to their high spirits with lavish quantities of wine from Montroig. With such treatment Ernst's overwhelming desire to see the paintings that surrounded them, turned to the walls, broke its bounds. With the help of his companions he proceeded to uncover all Miró's secrets. Becoming increasingly more aggressive, they finally invited Miró upstairs, where Ernst produced a rope he had used for mountain-climbing and, slinging it over a beam, placed a noose round Miró's neck in preparation to hang him. Questions were then put to Miró with sinister emphasis. 'Do you believe in God?' He replied evasively: 'I am not a philosopher.' Then, with more direct implication: 'Do you fear death?' He again replied: 'I am not a philosopher.' 'In that case,' said Ernst, 'if you are not frightened of death you are going to be hanged.' At a signal given by one of his friends, Ernst started to pull on the rope. But Miró's cunning was not only in his replies; he thrust his hands between the rope and his neck, and the noose slipped innocently over his head. With a sense of relief that the clowning had not finished in disaster, they allowed Miró to leave in a hurry; according to Ernst, he was not seen again for three days.

Boisterous behaviour of this kind could not, however, destroy the profound appreciation that both artists had for one another, nor did it rule out the possibility of working together. On the suggestion of Picasso, they had been invited in 1926 by Serge Diaghilev of the Ballets Russes to collaborate in designing the costumes and scenery for a ballet, *Romeo and Juliet*, with music by Constant Lambert. Their acceptance caused an abrupt reaction among certain surrealists, in particular Breton, who considered such activity to be frivolous and contrary to the serious anti-bourgeois principles of surrealism. As a result, and in accordance with the prevalent taste for agitation, there was a violent demonstration in the theatre on the first night. This was followed by a declaration signed by Aragon and Breton, beginning 'It is inadmissible that thought should be at the command of money', which was published in *La Révolution surréaliste*, the review edited by Breton which had frequently reproduced paintings by both Miró and Ernst. It now denounced them for their 'attitude which provides the worst partisans of dubious morality with weapons'.[14]

However, thanks to the loyalty and the more discerning influence of Paul Eluard, the following issue of the review included paintings by Ernst and Miró again, with a declaration initialled by Eluard: 'It will be necessary once more for us to recognize ourselves and our enemies, once more the latter must forgo their judgment of us.... We live in an atmosphere which for them is unbreathable. The most pure remain with us.'[15]

Eluard remained throughout his life an intimate friend of Miró. He was highly sensitive to the visual poetry in the work of his friend, and owned many of his paintings. Frequent collaboration between them culminated in 1958 in a rare and beautiful edition of Eluard's poem *A Toute épreuve*, brilliantly illustrated with coloured woodcuts by Miró.[16]

The two years during which Miró was based in the rue Tourlaque came at a time when the early heroic period of surrealist activity was reaching its highest point of animation. The usual meeting-place, where lengthy discussions took place every evening, was in some chosen café such as the Cyrano in the place Pigalle, or the Café de la Place Blanche. There was a continuous and lively exchange of ideas and projects covering a wide area from politics to new editions of poems, and embracing any idea, person or object that revealed some unheard-of peculiarity, or awakened a sense of the marvellous. Round the dominant presence of Breton, the progress and policy of surrealist activities was decided, exhibitions were planned, manifestos were written and signatures demanded. To refrain from signing was often interpreted as a lack of solidarity with the group, and at times this would be followed by a form of excommunication.

In their attack on classical aesthetic theories of ultimate or absolute beauty, it was probably Breton's emphatic statement that 'Beauty will be CONVULSIVE or will not be' that carried with it the most far-reaching implications. It heralded the violence that had suddenly appeared in 1925 in that great painting *The Three Dancers* of Picasso, and in his subsequent work; it became the basic attitude in all forms of surrealist expression and had an increasing effect on the work of Miró.

In contradiction to what may appear to be a tyrannical attitude when principles were concerned, the surrealists encouraged a wide variety of expression within the exceptionally talented group of painters that had been attracted towards them. Unlike the production of former movements – impressionist, Fauve or cubist – whose artists can be identified by a certain 'family resemblance', the works of the surrealists, as Patrick Waldberg points out, 'are from the first differentiated to such a degree that not even a temporary confusion is possible between an Ernst and a Miró, for example, or a Tanguy and a Magritte.... What they do have in common, nevertheless, is the desire, overthrowing all barriers, to reach that "beyond painting" that Max Ernst proclaimed as his goal.'[17]

A combination of Miró's retiring nature, his preference for solitude rather than the agitated company of his surrealist friends, and his admission of the value of diversity, made it possible for him to remain aloof and yet keep a close association with the surrealist group.

True to his habits, Miró returned every summer to Catalonia, and on 12 October 1929 he married Pilar Juncosa, who came from an ancient Majorcan family. On their return to Paris, Miró moved from the rue Tourlaque to a small apartment, 3 rue François Mouthon, in a remote quarter where, owing to the financial slump which again reduced artists to very humble circumstances, he was obliged to work without a studio. Two years later their only child, a daughter, Dolores, was born in Barcelona.

The two years spent in the rue Tourlaque had been immensely productive. Miró had worked so hard that there had been little time free for visits to the café, but even so he had kept up contact with his friends among the surrealists. In the spring of 1928 he paid a short visit to Holland, where he became intrigued by the detailed realism of seventeenth-century Dutch genre painting. On his return to Paris, bringing with him postcard reproductions to remind him of the originals, he painted four pictures in which his own sense of reality

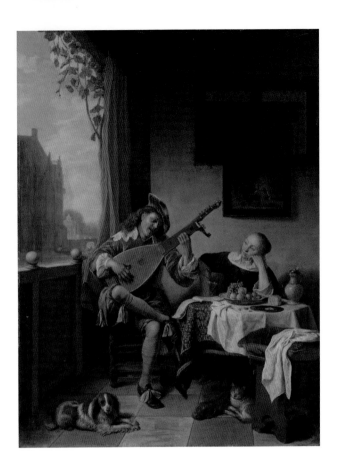

forms a strange contrast with the commonplace realism of
the Dutch masters. Although it is possible to trace the overall
arrangement of the original works, the liberties taken by Miró
45 result in a completely new version. In *Dutch Interior (I)*, the
dog, the musician, the table and the cat in that sober painting
44 *The Lute Player* by H. M. Sorgh, have been transformed with
outrageous humour into a vertiginous dance. Colour, form and
the proportions of each object obey Miró's orders and are held
together only by his masterly sense of design.

46 A brilliant picture of his, *Potato*, also of 1928, had its origin in
a seventeenth-century painting of a woman. The central figure
is surrounded by the intense activity of small lively forms in
brilliant colour and precise detail, but their fantastic diversity is
held in control by Miró's sense of rhythm and his ability to vary
the scale of objects to fit his design and his interpretation. For
example, the smallness of the hand on the left is contrasted with

44 OPPOSITE Hendrik Martenszoon Sorgh, *The Lute Player,* 1661
45 ABOVE *Dutch Interior (I) (After Hendrick Maertensz Sorgh's The Lute Player),* 1928

46 *Potato*, 1928

the monstrous growth of the hand on the right, which has graven on its palm the pattern 'M', which, besides having a religious connotation, is common to most hands and happens also to be Miró's own initial. The potato here is both a woman and an image of the earth itself, the earth-mother and an object of devotion.

47   Other portraits derived from artists of the past, such as *Portrait of Mistress Mills in 1750* (1929) after George Engleheart, are treated

47 *Portrait of Mistress Mills in 1750,* 1929

with equal freedom, although certain traces of the original are always present, like ghosts. The contrast between the sober realism of the original works and his own extravagant fantasy helped Miró to answer the question: ought we to oppose reality to fantasy, or are they complementary parts of the same totality? He was able to prove that, through fantasy, he could establish a valid aesthetic reality, understood and enjoyed as such.

Chapter 3
'Assassinate Painting!'

In Miró's treatment of the Dutch masters there was an element of admiration, mixed with a touch of mockery at the pedestrian conception which underlies their search for reality. There seemed to be something radically absurd in an art which limited itself to a photographic resemblance dolled up with the artificiality of academic arrangement. The illusion which these painters were striving to create in the name of reality might be enjoyed, with a certain indulgence, but it contained a pitiful misunderstanding of the true meaning of art.

It was this feeling of profound dissatisfaction with conventional standards that had provoked the violence of the dadaists and caused Duchamp to add a moustache to the *Mona Lisa*. Miró was now to express it in his emphatic declaration that 'Painting has been in decadence since the age of the cavemen.' Rather than subscribe to the falsity of the contemporary attitude towards art, Miró declared that he wished to 'assassinate painting', and to prove he was in earnest he denied himself for a while the means of expression – paint and canvas – that he had shown he was able to use with such outstanding talent.

The 'dream paintings' of the mid-1920s had become insufficient as a means of expression for him. They had developed from the ideas and techniques of surrealism. The latent revolt in Miró, which had been incubating ever since his first contact with Dada, had not yet revealed itself sufficiently and now, by delayed action, was ready to explode.

The manner of the explosion was not, however, the extraverted blast of the militant anarchist. Miró's anti-art revolt was an inner, personal affair, in keeping with the slow contemplative movement of his own nature. The moment for this outbreak arrived in the winter of 1928–29 and, paradoxically, the thoroughness with which he interrogated

48 *Portrait of a Dancer*, 1928

his own motives, and the discipline he imposed on his natural talents, led to new discoveries and a widening of his means of expression.

Having abandoned for a while the richness of oil and tempera paintings, he turned to collage as a medium which was less conventional and demanded a change of style. It also provided new opportunities to exploit chance encounters between objects and forms. The juxtaposition of unrelated objects had already become a surrealist technique; in Miró's hands the shocks produced in this way brought about a change in the nature of the objects themselves, a metamorphosis and a shift in our interpretation of their reality.

A subject close to Miró's heart was always the Spanish dancer. The new variations he devised on this theme in 1928 are in themselves objects of extreme simplicity. Paul Eluard described one that pleased him particularly as 'a picture that one cannot imagine more naked. On a virgin canvas, a hatpin and a wing feather'; this was sufficient to astonish Eluard and to evoke a trail of erotic associations. Other versions went even further towards abstraction. They consisted of geometric shapes drawn or pinned on a plain background so that all signs of painterly skill have vanished. But it is important not to confuse this tendency with the intentions of artists such as Piet Mondrian, who used abstraction as the basis of a new aesthetic. The difference here is that Miró's work was derived from a subject, the Spanish dancer. The process of abstraction he used had as its motive a revolt against the conventional aesthetic qualities required for a work of art. His aim was to evoke images by simple means, whereas Mondrian and his fellow abstractionists were seeking to establish a new form of art according to the laws of aesthetics stated in geometric abstraction and divorced from all references to subject-matter. Miró was in fact invited by Mondrian to exhibit with his Abstraction-Création group and refused indignantly, explaining that he did not wish to join them in their 'deserted house'. 'As though', he told Georges Duthuit, 'the signs I transcribe on a canvas, since they correspond to a concrete representation in my mind, were not profoundly real, and did not belong to the world of reality!'¹

49 LEFT *Collage*, 1929
50 OPPOSITE *Untitled.
Drawing-collage*, 1933

His abstract constructions led to a series of collages into
which he introduced the popular imagery of postcards,
and which he often completed with line drawings. In these
Miró showed for the first time his delight in using textured
surfaces and his ingenuity in the choice of strange objects and
materials. By a denial of his natural ability to exploit colour
and form in the conventional way with paint on canvas he had
discovered a new means of expression.

'If we ask: who is Miró?', wrote Ribemont-Dessaignes,
'we ask at the same time: what is painting?' The crisis that
induced Miró in 1928–29 to abandon painting was another of
those upheavals of the spirit that have continued periodically

51 *Torso of a Nude Woman*, 1931

to challenge fundamentally his attitude towards art and, by implication, towards life in general. The 'assassination of painting' led him to turn his thoughts from the exquisite finish of his earlier work and to look for stimulus among objects of the lowest order. The metamorphosis that could be brought about by putting such things as a piece of old rope, or a rusty mattress spring, in contact with bright colours and painted figures of his own invention, was an act of creation worthy of his attention. Experiments such as these corresponded to his dissatisfaction with the time-honoured limitations of the picture-frame. The influence of the objects he invented could now be physically extended into the space round them. Also, a lack of concern with permanence offered a means of provoking an immediate reaction from the spectator. It was the beginning of an attitude which he described to Georges Duthuit in 1936: 'As you see I attach an increasing importance to the content of my works. To me, rich and vigorous material seems necessary to give the spectator a blow between the eyes at first sight, which must hit him before other thoughts can intervene. In this way poetry expressed visually speaks its own language.'[2]

Many of the objects that Miró made at this time have disintegrated, as he intended, but enough have survived for us to be able to receive from them that shock which he claims is an essential part of his visual language. In this way they are unlike the cubist objects of Picasso which, although they were fragile, relied on harmony of composition and coherence of meaning. They are also unlike the dadaist readymades of Marcel Duchamp, being, in surrealist terms, 'objects functioning symbolically' rather than 'objects of concrete irrationality'.

It was the gaiety and artful childishness of objects such as *Man and Woman* (1931) that seduced the dancer and choreographer Léonide Massine, and persuaded him to ask Miró to design the costumes and décor of his ballet *Jeux d'enfants*, which was first performed in Monte Carlo the following year.

During the same period, about 1930, there was another new development – a series of oil paintings on paper. The backgrounds are bright with large areas of luminous colour. Signs drawn with vigorous lines in works such as *Torso of a Nude Woman* (1931) are mysteriously related to a transparent depth in which they float. The paintings gain their ethereal substance by a contrast between forms with a strong determined outline and a luminous void, revealing a continuity with the earlier search for a sensation of limitless space.

Ever since Miró abandoned representational realism in the early 1920s he tended to use flat surfaces of colour as a means of illuminating clearly defined shapes. But in some small pictures painted on wood panels in 1932, he developed further a method by which the forms became interlocked and united in spite of violent changes of colour. As one shape passed across another, like the shadow of the earth during an eclipse of the moon, its colour changed abruptly. For instance, if a black square overlapped a red circle the area of their intersection would change, say, to yellow, thus giving a continuity and a transparency to both shapes. By this simple device it became possible to preserve an uncompromising brilliance of colour, and also to allow the shapes to remain unbroken. In addition, a sense of the third dimension appeared mysteriously in a strictly two-dimensional style.

This invention has been of great service to Miró. He has never used it as a rigid system, but with varied adaptations it has become one of the characteristics of his work. It evokes an experience which goes beyond purely aesthetic considerations. In it we find a statement of the mutual change that takes place when two shapes of different colour intersect each other. Unconsciously Miró was stating a natural phenomenon in his

109

51

52

own terms. He was reversing the effect produced by applying layers of primary pigments to a white surface, which results in black. The luminosity of these 1932 compositions comes from his instinctive understanding that areas of coloured light projected on to a white surface produce white when they overlap. Miró had obtained with opaque colour the effect that is produced by the interaction of luminous colour.

Speaking of Miró's invention as a decision of genius, André Breton wrote: 'It seems to me that it is in the simplicity and the rigour of the form-colour relationship, thus totally recreated, that the absolute originality of works such as this and the secret of their affirmation on the organic plane resides.'[3]

The cubists had devised a means of preserving continuity in objects when otherwise they would logically have become hidden behind other objects. This inevitably introduces a sense of transparency, as it does in Miró's method, but his purpose is different. The cubists were preoccupied with objects which they wished to analyse and reconstruct according to a new conception. Miró is interested in presenting us with shapes which have organic implications, but which are only remotely connected with objects. We shall see later the astonishing metamorphoses that he brings about.

The small paintings of 1932 are knit together like a mosaic of forms in primary colours; the anatomical shapes of head, arms, breasts and body, although freely distorted, are still recognizable as signs. In the early spring of the following year, however, Miró embarked on a totally different path, which was to result in one of his most significant achievements and a major development of his style.

Working in a very restricted space in the attic of his home in the Pasaje del Crédito, he began by cutting out illustrations from catalogues of hardware, mostly minute but precise engravings of tools, machines and other merchandise. He then

55, 56 pasted these at random on large sheets of white paper. These collages, which in themselves have wit and the evidence of Miró's innate sense of composition, then became the models or the raw material from which he drew his inspiration. From them he began a series of great canvases whose dimensions were such that, owing to the lack of space in the attic where he worked, he could only keep one on its stretcher at a time.

The collages brought about a change of identity in the objects themselves. They were no longer a guide to purchasers. In their scale and their positions the illustrations now had no practical relation to each other at all. They forfeited their original, obvious connection with reality. But an even more astonishing metamorphosis was to follow, when Miró began to use these

52 *Seated Woman*, 1932

collages as models for his paintings. If we now compare the
two, it is possible in each canvas to find clues from the shape
and meaning of each of the catalogue illustrations and to trace
references to their positions in the collage, although Miró
allowed himself complete liberty in the transformations he
made. There are occasionally definite signs, like wheels or a
rudimentary face or hand, that give clues to their origin, but
otherwise the transition from a hardware catalogue to the
mysterious signs in the paintings has become intentionally
very obscure.

'Assassinate Painting!'

53 TOP *Painting*, 1933
54 ABOVE *Composition (Painting)*, 1933

55 ABOVE RIGHT *Collage (Study for Painting, June 13, 1933)*, 1933
56 RIGHT *Preliminary collage for Painting 1933*, 1933

Of the great variety and the spontaneity of these paintings
53   there is no better example than *Painting* (1933), which belongs to
55   the Museum of Modern Art of New York. The collage in which
it originated is composed of isolated pieces of engineering
equipment scattered over a white sheet of paper. In every
case Miró began his canvases by preparing a background in
rectangular areas of sombre colours, purples or greens that
merge into each other and give only a blurred sense of horizontal
and vertical divisions. The forms he then superimposed appear
to float, dance, or embrace, detached from the ground in an
all-enveloping cave-like atmosphere. They have substance that
suggests a shadow play of dancers performing a mysterious rite,
or signs painted or carved on the walls of a cave by prehistoric
man. It is a long cry between these evocations and the machines
that sparked off Miró's collages, but there is no doubt that
the shapes have now gained for us the status of symbols. The
question remains, however: what connection do they have with
reality? What, in fact, do they signify?

'Assassinate Painting!'   **77**

Miró tells us clearly that he never sets out with the intention of creating a symbol. How is it, then, that he can fascinate us by inventing what we might call abstract forms that appear significant and somehow related to prehistoric signs? The explanation, to me, lies in the relation of these forms to the fundamental shapes of organic nature, its growth and its movement, and to the attractions and repulsions that result in the perpetual reproduction of life around us. We find archetypal precedents, in simple fundamental forms such as the spiral, the circle, the triangle and the more anthropomorphic violin shape, in the earliest known works of art. But the symbol appears in the first place to impose itself rather than to be consciously created.

It is by virtue of his profound sensibility that Miró is able to communicate by means of symbols. In doing so, he resembles our ancestors who unselfconsciously created a language of art which speaks to us in a way that is timeless and universal. His forms, like theirs, act as an incitement to the imagination without being attached to a meaning. 'It is signs that have no exact meaning', Miró told me, 'that provoke a magic sense.' The degree of power invested in these signs must, however, depend on the ability of the artist. When, like Miró, they possess the sensibility of a magician, they can proceed by whatever means they may devise, and will be able to create living symbols which will establish a new communication between people and between humans and the transcendental forces of nature – signs that give shape to our most compelling emotions: love, hate, confidence, fear.

The great canvases of 1933 are important apart from their content, as being some of the largest in scale that Miró had yet attempted, and as the source of a style which he was to develop in the great murals that followed. He found in them the path that was to lead away from the detail of his small-scale easel paintings to other media, such as tapestries and the ceramic murals that he was later to construct.

Peintures Sauvages

From a distance Miró had approved of the rebellious attitude of the dadaists towards society, but the surrealist revolution into which he had become absorbed after his first arrival in Paris was for him, primarily, an adventure in personal methods of expression. It was with reluctance on his part that he was at times drawn into the group activities of his friends, and it was not until the political climate began to deteriorate seriously, in the early 1930s, that a profound and violent reaction to political events took place in him.

57 *Woman*, 1934

In 1934, following the great compositions he had painted the year before in Barcelona, Miró made a series of pastels on special paper which suddenly spoke of new and terrifying experiences. The 'gaiety, sunshine, health – colour, humour, rhythm' which characterized his earlier work were transformed into a prophecy of the crescendo of horror that was to begin with the Spanish Civil War two years later. The biomorphic shapes in pure colour, which had moved in a rhythmic dance in the compositions of 1933, now became solidified into fierce embodiments of female monsters seen in brilliant colour. In this frightening mood Miró used the softness of pastel technique to accentuate by contrast the fierce grimaces and

57

the violent distortions of the figures. Setting aside the discipline of flat colours and shapes, he accentuated the roundness of the forms with acid colours and soft gradations. The appearance of this series of about a dozen pastels was the prelude to a long and powerful succession of paintings to which Dupin gave the name of *peintures sauvages* (savage or wild paintings). It becomes obvious from these pastels alone that Miró had been deeply affected by political events over which he had no control and about which he was compelled to unburden his disquiet.

In the paintings that followed, such as *Persons in the Presence of Nature* (1935), instead of a lyrical delight in nature, reflecting the assured tranquillity of peasant life, which Miró had formerly treated with roguish humour, we find a sinister foreboding. The sky becomes loaded with red and black. Orgiastic, hysterical dancing in paintings such as *The Farmers' Meal* (1935) supersedes the elegant ballet of *Carnival of Harlequin* (1924–25). It is rare that an artist can sustain with such invention a pitch of violence as acute as was now to be revealed. The paintings of 1935 and 1936 are small in size and many of them are painted on copper with detailed clarity. In all of them we find a world of conflict and absurdity inhabited by creatures of incredible ferocity, even though their titles, such as *The Two Philosophers* (1936), *People Attracted by the Shapes of a Mountain* (1936) and *Two Personages in Love with a Woman* (1936), sometimes suggest the contrary.

However, one small painting typical of Miró's mood is given a title which does not belie its content: *Man and Woman in Front of a Pile of Excrement* (1935). A grotesque and gaudy couple gesticulate in front of a black sky. Their apparent satisfaction can only be due to a monument on the horizon, framed in an aura of light, to which they point with pride, but which is no more than putrefaction of their own creation. The fact that this situation can be described in words does not diminish the combination of mystery and nightmarish reality. The candour and the bold accomplishment of Miró's statement miraculously render the repellent horror and cynicism of this fable acceptable, even enjoyable. The figures are stripped to their essential significant features and are impregnated with a humour so ferocious that they regain a primeval innocence. 'Miró's art', to quote James Fitzsimmons, 'offers one of those rare instances of a modern technique successfully adapted to primitive subjects. His sense of ancient mysteries, of the irrational, of magical powers that stand behind all things, forcing us to take a stand and accept the unacceptable... comes through with exceptional vividness and power in these *peintures sauvages*.'[4]

58 TOP *Persons in the Presence of Nature,* 1935
59 ABOVE *The Farmers' Meal,* 1935

60 TOP *The Two Philosophers*, 1936
61 ABOVE *Two Personages in Love with a Woman*, 1936
62 OPPOSITE *Man and Woman in Front of a Pile of Excrement*, 1935

The first group of small paintings was followed by other
forms of expression in which the violence of Miró's feelings
was expressed in a more abstract style: situations brought
about by disquieting encounters between objects such as nails,
knotted string, an old toothbrush, lengths of chain, a rusty
bedspring, a gas-ring, a log decorated with erotic signs. With
these insignificant pieces of scrap he achieved sometimes
an expression of light-hearted surprise and at other times
an uneasy sense of discord. A painting of April 1935, *Two
Personages*, is an example of Miró's power to intensify images
by overriding aesthetic considerations and using unexpected
materials – in this case sand, a piece of bark, a tangle of string
and other substances stuck to the picture.

In 1936 the Spanish Civil War broke out; Miró was not to
revisit Spain until 1940. He now found it impossible to contain
the disquieting marriage between charm and horror within
the small dimensions of the exquisite paintings on copper,
and switched abruptly to a very different manner, using large
panels of masonite of uniform size. With coarse materials,
casein white, tar, red ripolin, sand and gravel, he attacked his
panels with vigorous gestures, relaying his emotions directly
in a style which proved to be the precursor of 'action painting'.
Spontaneous and obviously aggressive, they are indicative, in
different terms, of the same inner torment which is expressed

63 ABOVE *Two Personages,* 1935
64 OPPOSITE *Rope and People, I,* 1935

'Assassinate Painting!'

65 *Painting*, 1936

in the earlier paintings on copper. In his return to a more abstract form of expression, there is no slackening of tension or lessening in the vitality inherent in the signs.

Miró's means of expression were manifold, and the continuing anxiety caused by the Civil War made itself felt in 1937 in two other works of great importance: *Still-life with Old Shoe*, a medium-sized painting, and *The Reaper*, a large mural.

It is evident from the *peintures sauvages* that Miró's apparent detachment, his constant refusal to take any active part in politics, was a defensive measure. Beneath his tranquil façade he felt acutely and almost with clairvoyance the sinister menace of Fascist domination which was now attacking his own country. The *Still-life with Old Shoe* is, in all his work, the most concentrated evidence of his attitude, and can in some ways, as James Thrall Soby (who owned it before ultimately gifting it to the Museum of Modern Art, New York) points out, be compared with Picasso's great expression of indignation in *Guernica*, painted the same year. Although they differ greatly in conception and in size, both paintings share a deep concern for the sufferings of the common people. Miró uses as his material the familiar essentials of life, an apple, a loaf of

66 *Still-life with Old Shoe,* 1937

bread, a bottle of wine, an old shoe, seen in an atmosphere of
catastrophe. Their shadows are thrown up on the clouds and
mingle with the sinister colours of a great conflagration. Each
object is given a dramatic interpretation. The apple is pierced
by the relentless prongs of a fork which descends on it like an
arm from the sky, the bottle in tattered wrappings is warped
and blackened as though by fire, the half-eaten loaf is dry and
unappetizing, and the old shoe has surrendered its usefulness
in disintegration. As in all paintings of this series, unlike Miró's
'dream paintings' and his later work, this calamitous situation
takes place on the ground. The painting of this dramatic image
of a world threatened by destruction was achieved by long
concentration in the seclusion of a small room in Paris lent to
Miró by his friend and dealer Pierre Loeb.

67   *The Reaper* was commissioned by the Spanish Republican
Government and painted in the summer of the same year.
It was placed in the Spanish Pavilion designed for the
International Exhibition in Paris by José Luis Sert, the Catalan
architect who later built Miró's studio in Majorca and the
galleries of the Fondation Maeght at Saint-Paul de Vence.
Picasso's mural *Guernica* was also placed in the same pavilion,

'Assassinate Painting!'   87

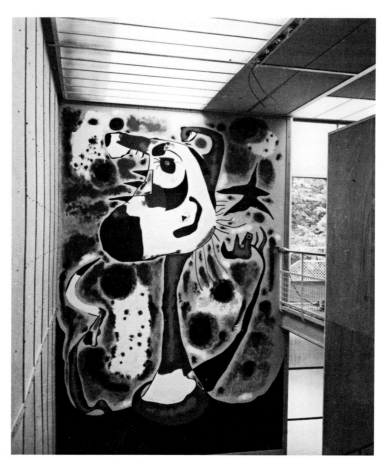

67 ABOVE *The Reaper*, Pavilion of the Spanish Republic, Exposition Internationale des Arts et Techniques dans la Vie Moderne, Paris, 1937
68 OPPOSITE *Aidez l'Espagne*, 1937

and near by was a *Mercury Fountain*, the work of another friend, Alexander Calder. The theme of *The Reaper* was again the Catalan peasant, treated with an exuberant violence which does not exist in those pictures of the same subject painted in the mid-1920s. In this case, a great head in profile, seeming to shout defiance, grew like a plant from the soil, crowned by a crumpled Phrygian cap and surrounded by a tattered star and large circular spots like explosions.

At the same time Miró produced a silkscreen print, in brilliant colour, with the words *Aidez l'Espagne*, 'Help Spain', written boldly round the figure of a Catalan peasant raising an immense clenched fist. The price of the print, one franc for Spanish relief, was worked emphatically into the composition.

All these public manifestations helped Miró to overcome his despair by presenting an image which is heroic, savage and not devoid of bitter humour.

As the Civil War continued, Miró discovered the means of living with his inner anguish. Four large paintings, each entitled *Portrait*, of astonishing brilliance in colour, and with a wonderfully inventive sense of form and a gay accompaniment of flaming suns and stars, were painted in 1938, as were other more light-hearted and poetic works such as *Une étoile caresse le sein d'une négresse* ('A Star Caresses the Breast of a Negress'). But there are two paintings of the same period inspired by women, *Head of a Woman* (1938) and *Seated Woman II* (1939), in which the full violence of Miró's feelings again makes itself felt.

70 ABOVE *Portrait No. I*, 1938
71 OPPOSITE *Head of a Woman*, 1938

There is a strange paradox in the contrast between the unfailing devotion of Miró to his wife and daughter and the extreme cruelty in the images of woman that he presents to us. The predominance of female symbols throughout his work is a clue to his preoccupation, but we never find him paying conventional tributes to Venus. On the contrary, particularly in the *peintures sauvages*, woman appears in a form which is diabolical and grotesque, closely suggestive of a bird of prey or a dragon, her attributes exposed like savage jewellery. Of all these images *Head of a Woman* is one of the most extreme in its violence. The blackness of the head, the ecstatic gesture of the arms thrown in the air, the stare in the bloodshot eye, the sparse bristling hair, the sharpness of the alligator teeth, the comic flaccidity of the nipples that protrude like tongues from open mouths, the combination of bird, animal and human being, and all this rising up in a blaze of colour before a deep blue sky, is a terrifying image alleviated only by the buffoonery of its convincing presence – a cruel comedy, so virulent that it transcends personal reactions and becomes the mischievous hieratic emblem of evil, splendid in its outrageous violence and belonging to the realm of dreams or of the gods.

71

Seated Woman II is a larger painting and again a fantastic image of mythical power. Like many of Miró's female symbols, the figure seems by the blackness of her form to belong to the night. Again the head is sinister and beast-like, and again there is great seduction in the fierce gaiety of the colour and in the eye-catching decoration of her breasts, which shine, isolated in the uniformly black shape of her body, as she bends threateningly towards us. By his savage wit Miró provokes us into reverence and admiration. Through his jungle of monsters we are led to the gateway of understanding. He invites us to feel delight and to cringe with terror, as we observe the female image, the form from which we emerge.

We find in these paintings, as we do throughout his later work, various metaphors for woman, by far the most frequent being the bird. There are some qualities common to both that are seductive, like the softness of down, the lure of colour, the grace of movement in dance and in flight, and the enchantment of song. In other pictures their attributes are diabolic, taking the form of sharp claws, teeth or beaks, such as we find in harpies or medieval devils. For Miró the bird is also frequently a symbol of movement, of flight, permitting a transference from one element to another, from earth to air. It is a sign of the depth and boundlessness of space, a means of transcendence. Its significance is such that it is not possible to limit the bird metaphor entirely to the female aspect. It often refers in Miró's 39 work to the male sexual act, as in the painting of 1927, *Un oiseau poursuit une abeille et la baisse*, and in certain references to the swan with its long, stretched neck and phallic beak.

For Miró the female, like the bird – *The Passage of the Divine Bird* (1941) is the title of the last of his wartime *Constellations* – has a fundamental connection with divinity. As the producer of life she is possessed of brilliance and authority. 73 She finds her place among the elements, standing before the sun, the moon and the stars or with birds in the night, and she is equally powerful as a symbol of darkness and of death.

Miró's entry into these regions is unpremeditated. His images spring directly from that universal realm described by Jung as the 'collective unconscious', rather than from any deliberate intellectual process of thought. Dupin adds: 'Miró finds again through painting the spiritual path of the mystics of all periods.' Far-reaching implications are born from the lightness of touch which makes his work both a simple delight and a profound experience. Woman and bird, substance and void, the obvious and the inexpressible, are brought within our experience.

Behind the cheerful, innocent, even tranquil look in his face, Miró was never immune to attacks of violent anguish

72 *Seated Woman II*, 1939

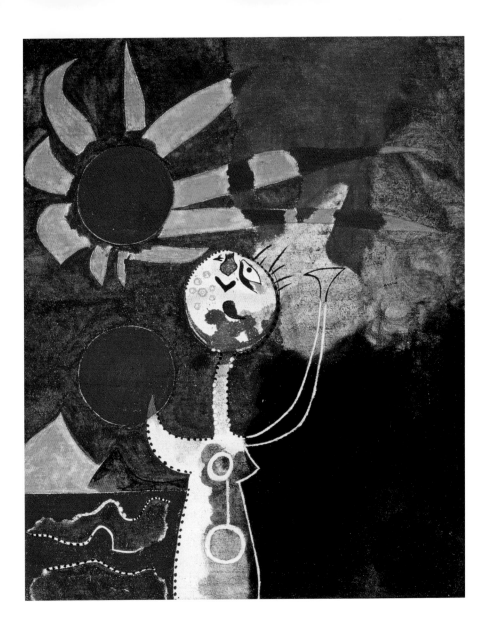

and depression. He was, however, always able to balance the threats of imminent disaster by equally potent forces. It was the ability to live with these tensions with comparative equanimity that gave his presence among others a unique quality and a sense of controlled power. He occasionally expressed this precarious condition in self-portraits, which, unlike the early representational work of 1919, that faithful likeness of his early naïveté, are metaphoric confessions of his inner life.

18

The later self-portraits, of which, apart from a few drawings, there are only three, began with an important work on which Miró bestowed a great deal of intimate thought. When he returned to Paris from Spain at the outbreak of the Civil War in 1936, he had again veered towards a degree of representation. We find this in the tragic realism of the *Still-life with Old Shoe* (1937) and also in drawings from the nude, among which *Woman Going Upstairs* (1937) is a powerful example of his capacity to distort the

74

66

73 OPPOSITE *Figure in Front of the Sea*, 1938
74 RIGHT *Self-portrait I*, 1937–38

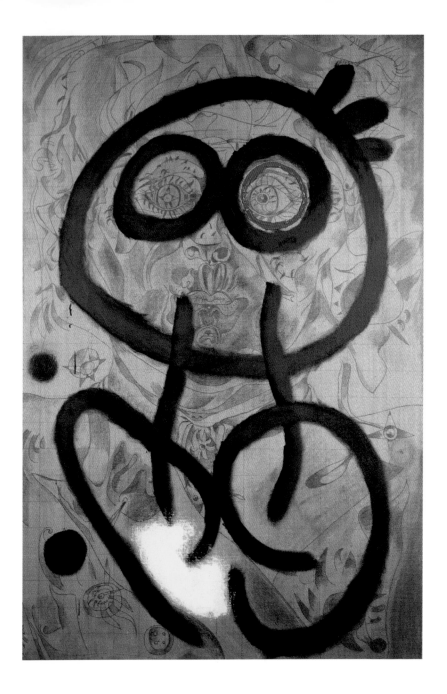

75 ABOVE *Self-portrait*, 1937–60
76 OPPOSITE *Self-portrait II*, 1938

female form with a cruel and violent humour; beside her we find once more, lightly sketched, a ladder, the symbol of escape.

Having again started to draw from life, he began a self-portrait as a pencil drawing from his image in a mirror. He worked on this for several weeks with the intention of turning it into a finished painting. Beyond a few touches of colour, it never arrived at this final stage; the result, however, was already a magnificent work which could not be more complete. Every detail gives evidence of his meticulous craftsmanship, of his introspective character, of the vision of an inner eye for which the horizon is the universe of his imagination, and of the depths of his disquietude. It is, to quote Dupin, 'a visionary portrait of a visionary painter'. The head appears to be enveloped in flames that do not consume it but emanate from it, and the eyes burn with an inner fire, like stars. He seems to exist in an atmosphere illuminated by suns, stars and comets, incandescent and explosive, but firmly holding his place in spite of their all-consuming power. Despite the lack of colour, this portrait literally achieves his desire that 'a picture should be like sparks. It should dazzle.'[5]

76   During 1938, Miró painted another image of himself in very different terms. On a black ground he placed two large flaming stars surrounded by other stars and cryptic symbols, thus

reducing the former introspective vision of himself to the single feature characteristic of the clairvoyant, the eyes.

More than twenty years later, in 1960, he again took up the same theme. After installing himself in his new studio in Majorca, he unpacked a large number of pre-war paintings and found himself in contemplation of the past. He had an exact copy in black and white made of the first self-portrait of 1937–38, with the intention of working on it with the detailed precision of a Mantegna, but as he examined it again his original idea evaporated; the obsessional character of his earlier work provoked a violent reaction in which his ironic sense of humour became decisive. In mockery of his former lyrical intentions he painted over the copy, with a heavy black line, a child's version of a head with three hairs sprouting from it, rising from a rudimentary body and neck. The only feature which is emphasized rather than overridden by this bold graffito is again the eyes, which are accentuated by circles that give them a ghoulish emphasis. The result is grotesque and disquieting. It is at least a convincing sign that modesty and continual self-questioning remained more characteristic of him than vanity. The treatment he gave to his former masterpiece was in fact similar to that which he applied on other occasions to colour reproductions of appalling banality: he transformed it, with complete freedom and innocent delight, into an entirely new work.

Chapter 4
War and Isolation

The Constellations

When the Second World War broke out, finding himself exiled from Spain, Miró left Paris and took a cottage, Le Clos des Sansonnets, in a very poetic spot near Varengeville-sur-Mer in Normandy, close to the house Georges Braque had built for himself some years before. They were old friends and continued to enjoy each other's company. Here a period of detached equilibrium began, in spite of increasingly sinister events.

Miró had with him an album which he had chosen because of the unusually beautiful quality of its paper. 'Materials', he wrote to me several years later, 'always excite me and give me points of departure of great richness.' He began, however, by painting several canvases influenced by the open landscape and birds in flight over the plain. In the same letter he explained how this led to his use of the album and the series of *Constellations* which forms one of the most brilliant episodes of his career.

77

78–82

After my work [on oil-paintings] I dipped my brushes in petrol and wiped them on the white sheets of paper from the album, with no preconceived ideas. The blotchy surface put me in a good mood and provoked the birth of forms, human figures, animals, stars, the sky, and the moon and the sun. I drew all this in charcoal with great vigour. Once I had managed to obtain a plastic equilibrium and bring order among all these elements, I began to paint in gouache, with the minute detail of a craftsman and a primitive; this demanded a great deal of time....

We had to leave Varengeville in haste. In this region which had remained calm the Germans opened up pitiless bombardments.

With the Allied armies completely defeated and continuous bombardments we took the train for Paris. Pilar took Dolores, who was then a little girl, by the hand and I carried with me under my arm the portfolio containing those Constellations *that were finished and the remainder of the sheets which were to serve for the completed series.*

We left Paris for Barcelona eight days before the entry of the Germans. We left there at once as a measure of prudence, and went to Palma where I could live peacefully, ignored by everyone and seeing nobody.

After this journey, in the catastrophic summer of 1940, in which the only possessions he could save were the *Constellations*, it was nearly three months before he was able to find sufficient tranquillity to take up the theme again with the 'rigorous severity' it demanded. His letter continued:

At this time I was very depressed. I believed in an inevitable victory for Nazism, and that all that we love and that gives us our reason for living was sunk for ever in the abyss. I believed that in this defeat there was no further hope for us, and had the idea of expressing this mood and this anguish by drawing signs and forms of which I had to be delivered on the sand so that the waves could carry them away instantly, or by making shapes and arabesques projected into the air as cigarette smoke which would go up and caress the stars, fleeing from the stink and decay of a world built by Hitler and his friends.

It must be very rare that a series of paintings that contain such coherence and lyricism should be completed in the midst of such catastrophic events affecting both the native country of the artist and the country he has adopted as a refuge. It is a sign of the fortitude and equanimity of which Miró was capable that his work continued unchanged in its quality and its impact. When by good fortune Miró was able to send the complete series to New York in 1944, it was greeted as the first artistic message to arrive from Europe since the fall of France. In his preface to the exhibition given them by Pierre Matisse, André Breton referred to the gravity of the situation: 'No, the condition of art (of great adventure and discovery) has never been so precarious as in Europe during the summer of 1940, when its days appeared to be numbered.'[1]

In the *Constellations* Miró showed once more his ability to revert to working on a small scale with minute detail soon after having produced paintings of monumental size. As their

77 *Flight of a Bird over a Plain II*, 1939

title suggests, they form a microcosm of life and movement
in space, interpreted by Miró with great sensibility. Our
perception of familiar events, and that of the immeasurable
arena of day and night that we inhabit, are blended together.
There is a unity of style throughout the series which recalls
the great compositions of 1933, but the scale is greatly reduced,
and titles (lacking in the 1933 paintings) are inscribed on the
back of each. Starting with backgrounds prepared with washes
of muted colour in the way Miró has described, they become
populated with his emblems, stars, circles, spirals, squares and
triangles, drawn with precision and illuminated with brilliant
primary colours wherever the organic or geometric shapes
intersect. Their poetic language is crystallized in titles such as
78 *Woman beside a lake whose surface has been made iridescent by a*
79 *passing swan*, or *Pink twilight caresses the genitals of women and*
80 *birds*, or, more simply, *Women encircled by the flight of a bird*.

But the charm of the titles and the enchantment of the colour are balanced by angry faces that can be detected fiercely showing their teeth; also there is a restrained rigour in the drawing of certain recognizable shapes such as eyes, stars, the crescent moon and a bold formal sign which Miró uses to designate the vulva, 'a Freudian heraldry of the Unconscious'.[2] Indeed, we find Miró here in his most seductive mood, using the full range of his talent. It is as though he had decided to condense all that he loves most, women, the night, stars, birds, dewdrops at dawn, into these small paintings, while emphasizing the precarious, illusory nature of our existence. Nostalgic themes such as *The nightingale's song at midnight and morning rain* are troubled by the appearance of grotesque masks that reveal Miró's underlying anxieties. He presents us with a world that is vast and richly furnished with good and evil. 'He allows us to penetrate into the cosmic order', writes Breton, 'with all that is involved in going beyond our condition.'[3]

In subtle ways, Miró alludes to his desire to evade the horrors that menace him. *The Ladder of Escape* is the title of an early *Constellation*, just as on 14 October 1940 he wrote on the back

81

85

78 OPPOSITE *Woman beside a lake whose surface has been made iridescent by a passing swan, 1941/1959*
79 RIGHT *Pink twilight caresses the genitals of women and birds, 1941*
80 BELOW *Women encircled by the flight of a bird, 1941*

81 TOP *The nightingale's song at midnight and morning rain*, 1940
82 ABOVE *People in the night guided by the phosphorescent tracks of snails*, 1940

of another: *The 13th, the ladder brushed against the firmament.*
Another is named *The Migrating Bird*, and the last of the series,
which began with *Sunrise*, is *The Passage of the Divine Bird.*
Perhaps the most expressive title, in circumstances from which
deliverance seemed so improbable, is *People in the night guided
by the phosphorescent tracks of snails.* Such hopes of salvation,
discovered in the intimacy of the night, could still be a comfort,
but the most ancient and infallible guide is known by Miró to
be found for ever in the constellations themselves.

Situated in time between the *peintures sauvages* and the
even more violent *Barcelona Suite* of fifty lithographs made in
1944, the *Constellations* have a measure of serenity which did
not return to Miró's work until after the war. For this reason
the series claims close attention; its poetic effect is greatly
enhanced by the titles, and by the prose poems of André Breton
which accompany each gouache in the facsimile edition.

The Barcelona Suite

Miró's unexpected return to Spain after four years in France
gave him the opportunity to rediscover, with fresh enthusiasm,
the landscape and the architecture of Majorca. In Catalonia as
a whole, the Gothic style developed local characteristics which
give it unique distinction in its proportions and its rigorous
control of ornament. The cathedral of Palma is a noble example
of this style, both in the warm colour of its masonry seen from
across the harbour and in the splendid proportions of its nave.
Such things were always important to Miró, and lie deep in the
instincts which governed his work.

During this tragic period when he lived unobtrusively in
Palma, he found satisfaction also in listening undisturbed
to music in the cathedral. As usual Miró reacted in a very
unconventional way, and to trace the direct influence of this
music on his work would be impossible, although there is
a painting of 11 May 1945 entitled *Woman Listening to Music,*
and another of the same year, *Dancer Listening to the Organ in
a Gothic Cathedral.* This latter might at least be expected to
provide an easy clue. But its main feature is the flourish with
which the line of a black arabesque dances across the centre
of the composition; and, although the line terminates in a
simple cross (a sign which for Miró does not necessarily refer to
Christianity), nothing else refers to religion in any conventional
way. The dancer is, however, flanked on both sides by grotesque
figures, one obviously female. They have expressions of dumb
piety or vicious nagging, while in the vault above floats a
third figure with a large open all-seeing eye. The painting is
as frankly pagan as any of Miró's Walpurgis Night fantasies.

The relationship to music must lie elsewhere than in Christian ceremony. It is more probably to be found in the circular shapes that, overlapping each other, retreat into the darkness like echoes, and in the vibration in the black line above them. In these signs we can feel a relationship between sound, space and colour such as Miró later established even more forcefully in

135

the painting *Silence* (1968). That this extra-pictural relationship is present is undeniable, but even so it does not constitute the main appeal of the picture, which is an immediate delight in colour and the movement that is implied by static visual means.

In 1942, Miró returned to his home in Barcelona, where, at last, the political situation had calmed down a little. His painting was limited by a shortage of materials and also by a desire to purge his style of the minute detail that had preoccupied him throughout the *Constellations*. Once more he turned towards new methods of expression. It was in 1944 that he began, with his friend Llorens Artigas, his first experiments in ceramics; he also became deeply involved in executing a series of fifty lithographs which have become known as the *Barcelona Suite*.

Miró has described how, on leaving Palma where he had worked with great precision and concentration on small, detailed paintings, he felt the need to liberate himself. 'Now I worked with the least possible control,' he told James Johnson Sweeney, 'at any rate in the first place, the drawing.'[4] Lithography in black and white gave him the outlet he needed to express with unchecked eloquence the violent emotions that had been subjected to severe discipline after the first outburst in the *peintures sauvages* and the great paintings of 1938–39. The *Suite* discloses the same anger which had been provoked by the continuous deterioration of the international situation before the war, but in its directness it is even more disturbing. That there should be a long period of gestation in Miró's ideas is not surprising. It is indeed characteristic of the way in which he allowed his ideas to develop subconsciously and reveal themselves with spontaneity.

84

The rapid technique of lithographic drawing suited Miró's mood. We find in the *Suite*, to quote Sam Hunter, that:

a ferocity of expression is here matched by superb control of composition and an astonishing richness of invention.... If anything, there has been a gain in psychological resonance and in the power to arouse disquieting emotion. Characterization and plastic expression register simultaneously, fulfilling Miró's express aim of reaching the spectator with 'an immediate blow between the eyes before a second thought can interpose'.[5]

83 *Dancer Listening to the Organ in a Gothic Cathedral,* 1945

84 *Barcelona Suite IV,* 1944

The absence of colour allows Miró to concentrate on the eloquence of his line, and on his power to use black in all its shades to supply texture and dramatic effects, but it is in the unbridled freedom with which he uses signs of his own invention to describe the monstrous activities of men and women that these lithographs excel. Nor does he allow himself to lapse into tortured expressionism. His vocabulary of signs transposes the effect of despair to one of angry humour. Grinning teeth and horn-like mustachios introduce a sense of comedy and childish fantasy. The monsters delight us by their absurdity, and the 'black humour' of the nightmare becomes a fascinating make-believe in which our most primitive emotions are exalted.

The *Suite* is one of the most convincing examples of the power of Miró's signs. They are presented in a stark, compelling way. Eyes, which often occupy the greater part of a face, or appear in the void, catch our attention by their irresistible power of penetration; teeth, lining open jaws, pierce and wound; limbs, breasts, wings carry their parent bodies in space so that they float, fly, or dance without any contact with the ground beneath them, their sexual organs candidly exposed. Never before had Miró been able to expose so spontaneously the depths of his agony.

85 *The Ladder of Escape*, 1940/1959, plate II from the *Constellations* portfolio

Chapter 5
New Horizons

In 1944 the death of Miró's mother resulted in the sale of the apartment in the Pasaje del Crédito, which Miró had been using as a studio since his return from Palma. Another event that heralded important future developments was the dispatch of the *Constellations* to New York through the help of a South American diplomat, and their exhibition the following year at the Pierre Matisse Gallery.

78-82

For four years Miró had not painted in oil on canvas, but his return to this technique took place with great ease and profusion. Continuing to prepare the ground with a variety of materials, he also began to use unconventional shapes for his canvases. Long narrow strips were used horizontally or vertically; along them signs could be read as a phrase from a new visual language. Other canvases were irregular in shape, or had frayed edges that dissolved into the space round them. The signs also developed a tendency to become more calligraphic and ambiguous, with resemblances to both hieroglyphic and alphabetical scripts.

At last, in 1947, the period of isolation came to an end. Miró was able to make a first visit of eight months to New York, where his work had received wide recognition since the retrospective exhibition of 1941 at the Museum of Modern Art. There he met Yves Tanguy and Marcel Duchamp, his surrealist friends, and Alexander Calder, whose drawings and mobile sculptures always had an affinity with his own work. He also found in New York his compatriot José Luis Sert, the architect who was to build the studio near Palma in which he would later work.

Hearing of his arrival, the directors of the Terrace Plaza (now Hilton) Hotel in Cincinnati, Ohio, asked Miró to paint a ten by three metre mural in the hotel restaurant. This was a commission directly in line with his desire to express himself on a large scale in a place frequented by the public. He spent a large part of his time in New York working diligently on etchings at S. W. Hayter's Atelier 17, where he astonished his friends by the enthusiasm with which he entered into new experiments in technique. It was there that he produced the etchings for a book of poems by Tristan Tzara, *L'Antitête*.

Being very much alive to his surroundings whenever he travelled, Miró reacted deeply to the atmosphere he found in the United States. The vitality and youth of its life, the vast scale of its architecture and landscape, the lights of its cities and the blatancy of its advertising, were the first factors that struck him, and brought exhilaration; but, even so, no obvious sign of these influences showed in his work.

Leaving America in 1948, Miró returned to Paris after an absence of eight years. Here again he received a warm welcome from his old friends. The year before, he had contributed some important works to a surrealist exhibition organized by Breton and Duchamp at the Galerie Maeght, and his friends the poets – Paul Eluard, Raymond Queneau, Georges Limbour, Maurice Raynal and others – expressed with eloquence their pleasure on seeing him back.

His visits abroad had provided Miró with a new stimulus. During 1949 and 1950 he produced a great quantity of paintings in two opposing styles, those on which he worked with concentration and perfection of detail – 'slow paintings', Dupin called them – and others which were astonishing for the urgency of their invention – 'spontaneous paintings'. In both cases the initial preparation of the background took place in advance, and Miró rarely showed greater science and sensibility than in this practice.

In the 'slow paintings' the signs and the general composition were developed with painstaking application and an attention

23   to detail such as he had given formerly to works like *The Farm* (1921–22) and the *Constellations*. Returning to them again and again, he would correct every feature until an impression of absolute finality was achieved. The forms and lines have great precision, and the brilliant primary colours of his signs, in which white and black also play an important role, produce an astonishing liveliness and luminosity which may be seen in

86   such works as *Women and Bird in the Moonlight* (1949), now in the collection of the Tate, or *People in the Night* (1950).

In this series of 'slow paintings', as in the compositions of 1933, Miró seldom gave titles to the works. As Dupin explains: 'The subjects of the pictures become effaced, they are no more than a pretext, or the accompaniment that sustains the melody.'[1] The paintings are a splendid example of complete

86 ABOVE *Women and Bird in the Moonlight*, 1949
87 OPPOSITE *The Blaze of the Sun Wounds the Lingering Star*, 1951

accord between the signs and the background, which is often
enriched by the addition of textured surfaces built up or
scraped down until there is a complete unity between the deep
atmospheric recessions and the animation, in line and form,
of the signs that appear to float in the foreground.

87

In the 'spontaneous paintings', which he was doing at the
same period, Miró gave complete freedom to the ingenuity
with which he was so well endowed. It was another proof of
his ability to use methods widely opposed to each other with
equal success. The 'spontaneous paintings' are surprising in
the diversity of the materials used, and in the invention of new
forms which add to the family of his signs. Backgrounds are
often heavily textured, with wire and string incorporated in
the composition. In many cases the signs seem to melt into
vaporous mists in the background or combine with splashes of
colour thrown at the canvas, a method which was to be taken
up by other painters and labelled *tachisme* a few years later. The
exquisite exactitude of outline, and the clear primary colours,
of the 'slow paintings' are replaced by vigorous arabesques in
which it is a delight to follow the line as it changes in emphasis
and direction. To trace its course is in every case a dramatic
experience; thus, some lines which have moments of bold swift
movement, in which the physical action of the hand is evident,
travel on to become blurred and absorbed into the background.

Again, Miró was usually not interested in giving titles to these paintings. The urgency which makes itself felt throughout puts them into the category of works which must be enjoyed for the freshness of their improvisation. Although their spontaneity makes it inevitable that some are more satisfying and significant than others, the whole series constitutes one of Miró's major achievements, which is enhanced by the contrast with the more deliberate, measured clarity of the 'slow paintings'. An admirable example can be found in the 1950 picture, now in the Van Abbemuseum in Eindhoven, in which Miró has used knotted cords breaking through a background of frenzied colour and varied textures. In this tempestuous atmosphere float creatures drawn with the precision of those of the 'slow paintings'. Others, however, such as *Woman in*

88

89

88 OPPOSITE *Composition with Strings*, 1950
89 ABOVE *Woman in Front of the Sun*, 1949

90 *Painting*, 1953

Front of the Sun (1949), are purely spontaneous and enjoyable,
like the movement of an unpremeditated dance.

The rich variety that followed after the divergent trends of
1949–50 was due largely to the freedom of action that Miró
was now able to combine with the detailed calculation which
had been an essential condition of the 'slow paintings'.
Titles adding their lyricism to the works again made their
appearance, and the methods and materials used for the

integration of signs into the mysterious depths of the
background became even bolder and more surprising.

Opportunely, Miró was commissioned in 1953 to paint a
very large picture for the Solomon R. Guggenheim Museum in
New York. For the first time he worked on an immense virgin
canvas without preparation or previous studies, and in spite
of this change in his methods he achieved a combination of
spontaneous freedom with an impressive display of powerful

New Horizons   119 forms. The ferocity of this painting recalls in a brutal manner the monsters of the *peintures sauvages* (see Chapter 3), but the violence is now contained in the manner in which the forms are painted rather than in their individual expressions. The method used here is the antithesis of the calculated precision of the signs and figures of the 'slow paintings'. There is a complete disregard for delicate refinements. Instead, there is a 'fecund clumsiness', a direct and brutal assertion of the inner energy that the painter has succeeded in liberating. Stains, accidental blotches of paint and crude, hasty brushmarks contribute to the urgency of the message that is being proclaimed. Even the portentous assurance and overwhelming proportions of the central figures become ambiguous and are absorbed into a splendid display of transmuted emotion. Against the confused vaporous colouring of the background the massive red and blue form of the dominant figure makes an impressive contrast.

The savage element is not absent in smaller paintings of this period, such as *Woman Struggling to Reach the Unattainable*

91 BELOW *Hope Comes Back to Us as the Constellations Flee*, 1954
92 OPPOSITE *The Half-Open Sky Gives Us Hope*, 1954

(1954). Here once more Miró renounced all grace and lyrical charm in favour of a more direct form of expression in which the unembellished gesture is made to speak. There are other paintings in which biomorphic signs tend to become obscured and the movement and colour of more indeterminate graffiti become increasingly eloquent. In the painting *Hope Comes Back to Us as the Constellations Flee* (1954), the phantoms of symbols become faintly entwined in a luminous primeval fluid. Three black elliptical shapes punctuate the composition like large holes pierced through to infinity or, indeed, like eclipsed suns travelling over the surface of the painting. The ambiguities of depth are accentuated by the reassuring imprint of hands scattered over the surface of the canvas, of which we should otherwise cease to be conscious. In another version of the same theme, *The Half-Open Sky Gives Us Hope* (1954), depth and atmosphere are established by a fantastic choice of techniques applied with what appears to be unrestrained brutality. The blackness of the background has been fiercely worked by scratching, rubbing and the addition of textures in casein. Again handprints appear, now white against a fathomless darkness, as a reminder of the surface of the canvas.

Later Years

Miró always had a desire to branch out from the high road of painting into other media, and to re-establish a connection with the public, independent of the conventional contacts through dealers and museums. Between 1954 and 1959 he devoted much of his energy to ceramics and to lithography and engraving.

In 1959 Miró again visited the United States at the time of a second retrospective of his work in New York, at the Museum of Modern Art, and also in Los Angeles. International recognition of his genius had already begun when he was awarded the Grand Prize for Engraving at the Venice Biennale of 1954; and in America, where appreciation of his work was far in advance of Europe, he received the Grand International Prize of the Guggenheim Foundation from the hands of President Eisenhower.

Miró often claimed that he preferred to work in discomfort. The bohemian squalor of the rue Blomet was overcome by whitewash and his systematic tidiness. The cramped quarters at Montroig and the Pasaje del Crédito, where he had literally to crawl under his canvases on his belly, never impeded the freshness of his inspiration nor the quality or quantity of his work. But a combination of circumstances – a house among olive trees on a hillside at Calamayor near Palma with a splendid view of what then was an unspoilt coast, his lifelong friendship with José Luis Sert, and a half-suppressed wish that Miró had expressed when he said in 1938 'I dream of a large studio'[2] – these factors persuaded Miró in 1956 to commission his friend to build for him a studio among the terraces and olive trees of Calamayor. This combination of Miró's needs and Sert's understanding produced excellent results. The siting, the appearance, external and internal, the lighting and the functional qualities were admirably conceived. But as might have been foreseen, Miró had difficulty in adapting himself to an atmosphere of such perfection, and more than two years passed before he was able to establish himself there at all. It was only in 1959 that he was again able to paint, and a new period of activity began.

A few years later, in order to satisfy his need for close contact with the peasant life of the past, he bought a neighbouring farmhouse of splendid eighteenth-century proportions built of the local golden-coloured stone. In the white-washed emptiness of its lofty rooms he was able to withdraw, meditate and wander among the stacks of canvases and found-objects in all stages of achievement and metamorphosis.

The completion of the new studio brought an important consequence. Since his flight from Paris in 1940 a large quantity of half-finished canvases and objects had remained in store. It was now possible for Miró to see them again, and with great concentration he sorted them out. Some were rejected, but others he judged could receive further attention, although the idea of completing a work in the same spirit as that in which it had been begun some thirty years before was inconceivable. Although Miró often worked on a picture over a very long period, he never retouched them. When he returned to a previous work he used it in an impersonal way as the point of departure for fresh inspiration. A painting which illustrated his

75   mood on recovering his pre-war work is the *Self-portrait* begun in 1937, the treatment of which I have described in Chapter 3.

93   In *Swallow Dazzled by the Flash of the Red Sloe* (1925–60), it is difficult to find traces of the original, but the finished painting without doubt owes its richness to its past history and offers a proof of the continuity in Miró's work and his power of renewal.

The new studios opened for Miró the possibility of expansion, and not only in a physical sense. We have already seen how he often chose to work in opposite modes and to vary the media of his expression constantly. The additional space of the studios gave scope to the sense of orderly development and continuity which was a fundamental basis of Miró's work, just as the soil on which he walked was the springboard for the flights of his imagination. There was thenceforth always to be more than one trend to follow in his work, and at times they would even appear to be diametrically opposed. The new studio, only a few yards from his house at Calamayor, became the centre of painting, still the focus of all his activities; and, with this and the more primitive house higher up the hill, he was furnished with all the space and the means he needed for painting and the germination of ideas which were later worked out in other forms elsewhere – at the foundry in Barcelona, the kilns of Gallifa and the workshops and presses in Paris and Saint-Paul de Vence.

After his return to painting in 1959, simultaneously with the execution with Artigas of a ceramic mural for Harvard University and continued production of graphic works, Miró found himself working out new paths, characteristically varied in direction, in his studio at Calamayor. A series of small canvases identical in size, known as the *Fonds blancs* ('white grounds'), revealed a new tendency. In the first group, nebulous shapes move in an atmosphere of impenetrable mist. In the second, over the same deep white cloud, disconnected lines have been rapidly scribbled on the surface with a disregard

93 ABOVE *Swallow Dazzled by the Flash of the Red Sloe*, 1925–60
94 OPPOSITE *Woman and Bird II/X*, 1960

that could be called 'anti-drawing', giving an effect of depth similar to the handprints of the paintings of 1954. A third group has an even greater degree of abstraction. The white ground is marked by bold splashes of black paint thrown at its surface so that the gesture of throwing becomes imprinted and frozen. At the same time Miró was making a series in which, with a bold precision characteristic of his fluent calligraphy, he painted signs using a thick brush full of black paint on pieces of coarse hessian cut from old sacks. The sacking was otherwise left bare, and commercial lettering stencilled on the sack became part of the composition. The signs, developed from his symbols of birds and women, are recognizable by their movement, but the chief delight of these small works lies in the primary colours sparingly used to solidify certain shapes, the nebulous spots of colour in the background, and the conviction of the line that delineates the forms and dances round them.

94

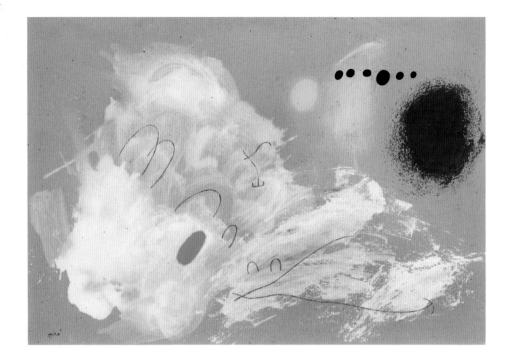

Another very different mood accounts for a large number of paintings on thick sheets of cardboard, a material which attracted Miró by its banality, and on which he exerted every means, such as tearing off corners, gouging out patches and holes, soaking it to make it warp, and adding rich textures to bring its sluggish surface to life. Again, as with the 'spontaneous paintings', the results vary in quality. His triumphs are those in which there is a metamorphosis. The unattractive disintegrating material itself becomes an imposing mass, the vehicle which carries the bold and vital indications of life given by the colour and signs bestowed on it by Miró.

Just as Miró exalted the meanest of materials in paintings on cardboard or other pieces of rubbish, such as fragments of fibro-cement, that attracted him by the banality of their shape, so at other times he used the blots made at random on a canvas, interpreting them with a minimum of signs, and with colour applied with the same haphazard appearance. These touches owe their significance to the mysterious precision with which they have been placed, and the tact with which they enhance rather than alter the original stain. In such paintings, 'the blot itself possesses a significant power in Miró's creation', writes Dupin. 'It illuminates slowly the genesis of forms and

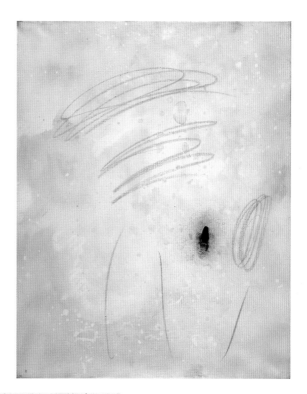

95 OPPOSITE *Solitude III/III*, 1960
96 RIGHT *Painting I/V*, 1960
97 BELOW *Painting II/V*, 1960

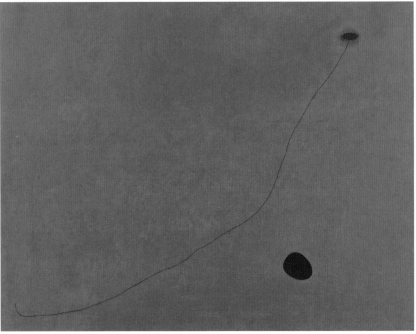

98 TOP *The Red Disc*, 1960
99 ABOVE *Blue III*, 1961

figures beginning from the raw material, supreme and blind, that contains the vital energy without which the effort is no more than another stage towards the inevitable return to the material itself.'³

Experiments such as the *Fonds blancs* were to lead to new developments in Miró's conquest of space, a preoccupation that we have noticed in his work as early as the blue 'dream paintings' of 1925. It was now to find its expression on a much greater scale in three paintings of 1961, *Blue I, II, III*.

33

99

Miró was now to forgo all the enchantments of his signs and symbols and concentrate only on the liberation of the spirit in space. These three great canvases of limitless blue mist owe their sensation of depth to black spots and bars of brilliant red which hover in the foreground, close to our eyes. Also, in two of the paintings a tenuous black line like a kite-string crosses the canvas and penetrates deep into outer space.

In 1962 Miró pursued even further his intention of creating a sense of space with the simplest possible means in three large canvases entitled *Mural Paintings for a Temple: Yellow, Green, Red*. Denying even the nebulous play of colour on the canvas, and limiting all figuration to a few black circles and tenuous lines, he created an environment of pure colour for our contemplation, with rare focal points which can provide anchors for a hypnotic meditation. His purpose was not decoration but rather to offer a means of escape into the infinite, for which the ladder in former paintings had been a symbol.

The deliberate elimination of signs and of all traces of representation in these canvases would appear to bring Miró dangerously near to pure abstraction, which in the past he had violently rejected as a means of expression. As we shall see, however, by an even more stringent application of the same process, he would go on to produce a triptych of great purity and significance a few years later, the *Mural Paintings for a Hermit's Cell* of 1968.

It was evident from the great retrospective exhibition held in 1968 at the Fondation Maeght and later in Barcelona, and in 1969 in Munich, that the quantity and variety of Miró's output in the preceding decade was prodigious. But beyond this remarkable achievement is the progress towards new powers that Miró was able to incorporate into whichever mode of expression he was using. In the great exhibition in Barcelona, the works dated 1968 amounted to over sixty paintings, the majority being of large dimensions, twenty-eight graphic works and over thirty sculptures, mostly in bronze.

It might be thought that such an astonishing output could lead to repetition and weakness due to haste, but the mastery Miró attained in so many different forms of expression and the richness of his imagination saved him from any such reproach. In the 1968 paintings he developed new methods. There are those in which the gesture of his hand and the dramatic sensitivity of line are supreme. Vigorous examples of this are *Words of the Poet* and *Poem III*. In both paintings the effect relies above all on the flourish of a line punctuated with spots of bright colour which, as we follow it, speaks a dramatic language with continuous eloquence. The same applies to the family of signs and arabesques which covers the canvas in *Dance of People and Birds Against a Blue Sky; Sparks*. An equally astonishing flight of stencilled letters and numbers appears in *Letters and Numbers Attracted by a Spark (I)*. The ground of liquid red on which they cluster is broken into by the explosion of green fire. Unlike early paintings in which the letters spelt out a word or even the artist's own name, here they are depersonalized, abstracted from an exact interpretation so as to be read as a mysterious language which he helps us to invent for ourselves.

100, 101

103

102

100 BELOW *Words of the Poet*, 1968
101 OPPOSITE *Poem III*, 1968

New Horizons

102 LEFT *Letters and Numbers Attracted by a Spark (I)*, 1968
103 BELOW *Dance of People and Birds Against a Blue Sky; Sparks*, 1968
104 OPPOSITE *The Gold of the Azure*, 1967

The painting of 1967, *The Gold of the Azure*, is a splendid example of Miró's ability to combine new forms with the exquisite calligraphy of signs and stars. The large transparent blueness of an isolated elliptical mass gives the sensation that the immensity of the heavens can be rolled up into one ball, floating in a golden atmosphere which is populated by indefinable creatures, and by the galaxies of outer space, red and green in the immeasurable distance.

There are other paintings in which Miró's attachment to the night and the nocturnal presences of women and birds is evident; but Miró does not see the night as darkness. For him, paradoxically, the happenings of the night are conceived in

a brilliant display of colour. The small painting *Woman and Bird at Night* (1968) is rich in primary colours, which create the background; the tall serpent-like form barring the centre of the picture – the woman – is black, as are the bird-like signs that fly round her. Miró, as usual, remains ambiguous in his use of signs, and the large white crescent that dominates the composition can be interpreted either as the moon sailing

105 LEFT *Woman and
Bird at Night,* 1968
106 OPPOSITE *Flight of
Birds Encircling the Woman
with Three Hairs During a
Moonlit Night,* 1968

through the sky or as a bird in flight. In this painting we find
a deliberate return to the symbolism of earlier paintings; the
signs, while they have gained a new lyricism, have become
more integrated into the composition.

106   Another triumphant tribute to the night is found in *Flight
of Birds Encircling the Woman with Three Hairs During a Moonlit
Night* (1968). Here the arrangement of the composition is
amazingly simple. Only three primary colours are used with
black and white. With the ingenious contrast of the white star
and circling birds, and the apparent distance created by the
curve of the green crescent moon showing light against a black
sky, a reversal takes place below as the black flows into the

border of the red circle, and the delicate tracery of stars and birds surrounding the sign of the woman moves in silhouette against the golden moonlight.

107 An earlier painting, *Woman Before an Eclipse with her Hair Dishevelled by the Wind* (1967), reveals to us the strength of Miró's style in the late 1960s. It can be compared with the 70 *Portraits* of 1938 in the economy of its means, but it also combines the spontaneity of Miró's later experiments in texture, which appear in the background, with a determined and yet sensitive structure, seen in the figure of the woman herself. There is an impressive sense of finality in the placing of the heavy black forms of the figure, contrasted with the

107 ABOVE *Woman Before an Eclipse with her Hair Dishevelled by the Wind,* 1967
108 OPPOSITE *Woman Encircled by a Flight of Birds in the Night,* 1968

108

careful drawing of the signs beside her and the sparse use of pure colours. In particular, the composition depends on the placing of the patch of yellow in relation to the green, and the red crescent tipped with blue. Keenly sensitive to the role of each colour, Miró often used yellow, as he does here, as the source of light in a picture, placing it last and giving it a role of essential importance. The authority that emanates from this painting is clearly the outcome of long experience and a struggle to situate the maximum of significance in a picture without lessening in any way the spontaneity of action which is necessary if the springs of the imagination are to flow freely.

Two important paintings of 1968 show once more the strength of Miró's desire to experiment with untried materials. In both cases he used large pieces of crumpled sailcloth with their cords still dangling from them and their holes and stains still apparent. *Woman Encircled by a Flight of Birds in the Night* (1968) is a piece of tarpaulin measuring more than three metres square. Miró discovered in it a background full of associations. He decorated it with a bold arabesque of bird signs, surrounding the serpent-like woman who moves across the bottom of the canvas. Her form is like the outline of hills, and rears up into the centre of the composition as it approaches the rays of a large black star. A movement following the creases of the canvas might have become facile, but he arrested it by placing with deliberation small squares of brilliant colour stuck to the canvas, and adding knots of cord in pairs like eyes in the night. There is again great sensitivity and skill in the way Miró used the crumpled texture of the background. The vast scale increases the ambiguity of the effect; the painting can appear like a wall of elephant hide, or open up and envelop us in a deep limitless space. It is a further example of the artist's masterly skill in the handling of uncouth materials and his mysterious power of creating depth.

Chapter 6
Sculpture and Other Media

Many of Miró's sculptures, as I have said before, evolved from the early surrealist objects which were made of unexpected combinations of elements. This process often involved the use of random discoveries among the insignificant objects, natural or artificial, that litter the world around us, waiting to be given a new life through the metamorphosis that Miró was able to bring about. He made sculptures built up of broken pots, old roots, limbs from celluloid dolls, sticks, electric bells and feathers, which come to life as projects for monuments to be constructed later in concrete, bronze or a mixture of materials. In spite of the meanness of the original material, a hieratic presence emerges; the transformation that has taken place brings a sense of elation that the spirit can be restored from such a heterogeneous collection of despicable trash. This process has been exploited by innumerable artists in recent years; but Miró had the rare ability to create each time a new conception which is entirely convincing in its own personality.

Miró admired greatly the traditional Catalan figures made in remote parts of Majorca, modelled in clay and usually painted, which have a resemblance to the archaic sculpture of indigenous peoples. The simplicity of their forms, in which can be felt the imprint of the fingers that modelled them, influenced him in many small works made in clay or plaster. Here also, Miró's symbols find a three-dimensional interpretation, becoming tangible and giving delight through the textures of their surfaces. The internal life that is enclosed mysteriously in their form, the signs incised on the exterior, as well as their colour, add significantly to their meaning.

Miró, as a skilled craftsman, had many ways of developing his ideas. Small constructed sculptures could become monuments, and the original ephemeral materials could

109 ABOVE *Man and Woman*, 1931
110 RIGHT *Poetic Object*, 1936

111 *Object of Sunset*, 1936

be cast in concrete, marble or bronze. In the great flow of
creative energy during 1968 that produced such riches in
painting and other media, there came into being a group of
bronzes in which Miró found the means of giving expression
to his artistic ingenuity.

Again, it was often the meanness of an object or a material
that attracted him and gave him a starting point. In a basket,
of the kind traditionally used in Mediterranean countries by
builders, he saw a head. The handles became its ears, and
drooping eyes and a snout were made from parts of a celluloid
doll. This assemblage was then mounted on a body which
has the appearance of being wrapped in a toga, in the lower
part of which a limb, again detached from a doll, protrudes
in an ambiguous gesture of greeting. This strange mixture of
objects finds a new unity by being cast into bronze. Under his
instruction, José Parellada, a young craftsman in Barcelona,
cast more than a dozen figures by Miró in 1968 and gave them a
patina which is admirably suited to the process of unifying the
heterogeneous ingredients.

112

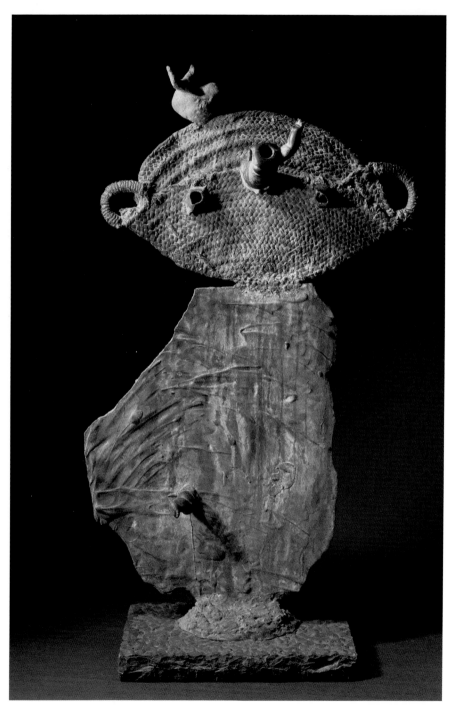

112 ABOVE *Figure and Bird*, 1968
113 OPPOSITE *Figure*, 1968

113   Another of these sculptures is cast from three elements. The two lower ones are irregular oval patches of clay set vertically, each bearing the imprint of a foot, and both supporting a square tile, on which has been incised a face with large round eyes and a highly equivocal expression. There is a choice as to how the figure is to be interpreted. The feet could equally well be hands, or perhaps a cloak enclosing the empty central area which becomes the body of a square-faced gentleman.

114   In *Woman* (1968), made with Josep Llorens Artigas, Miró relied more exclusively on the rough texture he gave to the original clay. The only extraneous materials used are stones embedded to emphasize certain points. The overall shape of the figure contains the ambiguity of the symbols that appear in the paintings. From the pear-shaped body in which two vertical rifts have been opened, suggesting the holes in a violin, rises a long neck with arms attached to it like the barbs of an arrow, giving the figure a curiously hermaphroditic appearance.

It was perhaps when at work on ceramics that Miró enjoyed most completely the full scope of his genius. There was no facet

114 LEFT Joan Miró and Josep Llorens Artigas, *Woman*, 1968
115 OPPOSITE Joan Miró and Josep Llorens Artigas, *Small Figure*, 1956

in the wide range of his talents that did not come into play, and in addition he was assisted by an old friend, Josep Llorens Artigas, who had shared his ambitions and disappointments ever since they met in Barcelona at the Sant Lluch circle in 1915, and who had since become an expert in the art of ceramics.

Artigas adapted himself willingly to Miró's astonishing career, with a desire to make it possible for the artist's most unconventional ambitions to be realized. He installed his kilns close to his house in the isolated village of Gallifa, on a mountainside near Barcelona. With a knowledge of Chinese and Japanese techniques, and the sensitivity of a man who has mastered all the refinements of his craft, Artigas made it possible for artist and craftsman to supplement each other's qualities as they worked together. He refused to install gas or electricity, and used only the wood from the forests to get the high temperatures he needed in his kilns.

Ceramics were for Miró an extension of both painting and sculpture, in which many of his discoveries in both arts could

115

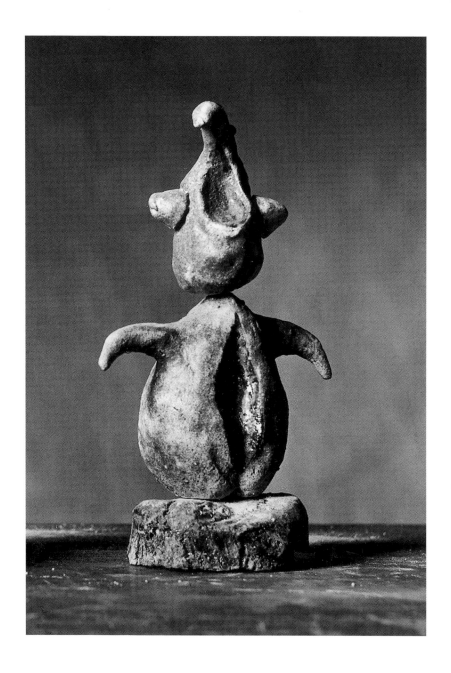

be combined. There was everything in this art to enchant him. It begins with the earth, the clay which can be modelled in the hands, pressed against an object or a surface so as to receive its imprint, thrown on a wheel so that it has both an exterior and an empty space within; its surface can be embellished with colour, texture and signs. The next stage is more dramatic. Fire now takes all into its control, and artist and craftsman stand aside, imposing their will only in so far as they are able. Miró was undismayed: the firing might by some unaccountable freak produce a result which was unexpected, but he was prepared, as in his paintings, to find ways of taking advantage of such happenings. He and Artigas worked with the elements, and the results bore the imprint of a profound understanding between themselves, and between man, earth and fire.

The literal fusion of sculpture and painting allowed Miró to use the primary colours which were significant in his painting and to gain three-dimensional effects in which paint is no longer an illusory medium evoking depth on a flat surface but part of a solid object which can be touched, and which can contain space as well as occupy it. The senses of sight and touch, which he so often combined in the illusions created by his paintings and collages, here unite, and Miró exploited the possibilities offered with great skill. In pieces such as *Large Figure* there are forms and surfaces which have clearly defined associations; the head in this case seems ancient and worn like a block of lava, whereas the body has the sharp roughness of a crudely woven garment. In other ceramic sculptures we feel the surprise brought about when a substance, such as clay that has been fired, is put together with other materials to form a unity. A presence such as this exists in *Woman* (1962); from its wooden body, which is flat and round like the cover of a barrel, rises a very long ceramic neck and head. In other hands, such sudden changes of material might strike us as merely incongruous, but with Miró's sensibility, and the sense of humour he shared with Artigas, they not only win acceptance but involve us in a mysterious metamorphosis. The bewildering success of these marriages of improbable materials is the result of Miró's ability to make use of anything that was at his disposal.

Whatever the medium used, there was always a close affinity in Miró's work to the natural forms around him. The powerful landscape of Catalonia had always been, he tells us, 'an essential element in my plastic and poetic conception'. He often found the stimulus he needed for his ceramics in actually painting directly on the surface of rocks which formed

116 OPPOSITE Joan Miró and Josep Llorens Artigas, *Large Figure*, 1956

117 LEFT *Woman*, 1962
118 OPPOSITE *Green Woman*, 1968

part of the mountain landscape. And when his colours, signs and surfaces became fused into a ceramic he enjoyed seeing them again in natural surroundings. They were at one with the landscape, a result which he knew would be impossible and ridiculous should he try to place a naturalistic painting against a mountain.

Cooperation with nature continued throughout. Miró did not make drawings in advance for his ceramics, and their variety of form is enormous: some are sculptures, others plates

118

and jars, others small precious objects, while others are made to take their place in architecture. When asked by Rosamond Bernier which of these many kinds he preferred, Miró replied:

It is always the last, the one just out of the kiln, about which I feel most strongly. Some of the new ceramics are very big. I have been working with a sense of the monumental, thinking of their possible incorporation in architecture. This could be the way to enrich workers' dwellings and no longer treat those who live in them as insensitive robots.[1]

120, 121

119

133

In other ways, ceramic art can approach painting more closely. In several places Miró created masterly designs for tiled walls, either isolated like those outside the UNESCO building in Paris, or as part of the architecture like those commissioned for the universities of Harvard in Massachusetts and St Gallen in Switzerland, where the design is a long, narrow frieze. In 1970 he completed a tiled wall of monumental proportions for the airport of Barcelona.

Monuments

Physically Miró belonged to a Mediterranean race who
are small in stature, but whose achievements are often
monumental. His capacity to produce so vast a quantity of
paintings, engravings, lithographs, ceramics and sculpture
reminds us of his compatriot Picasso. Although Miró paid
meticulous attention to detail in his work, he always had a
strong desire, and the ability, to express himself on a very large
scale. The easel picture appeared unsatisfactory to him for two
reasons. It does not offer a physical sense of environmental
space, nor can it be incorporated appropriately into architecture
and public places. As early as 1938 he wrote: 'I want to try, in
so far as possible, to go beyond easel painting, which in my
opinion has too mean an aim, and get nearer in painting to the
masses of whom I have never ceased to be aware.'[2]

Before the war, large-scale designs for the ballet, cartoons
for tapestries and decorations for the children of his friend,
the architect Paul Nelson, gave him the possibility of showing
that the strength and simplicity of his style could be admirably
adapted to monumental design.

67   One of the largest paintings was the great mural, *The
Reaper*, commissioned for the Spanish Pavilion in the Paris

119 *Mural Painting*, 1950–51

International Exhibition of 1937; placed at the top of a flight of steps, it filled a whole wall. But owing to the misfortunes of war it disappeared mysteriously when it was sent to Spain at the close of the exhibition.

It was not until after the war that the opportunities he was hoping for offered themselves in America. In the Cincinnati mural of 1947, and in the smaller one for Harvard Graduate Center (1950–51, now in the Museum of Modern Art, New York), the candour of Miró's brilliant unshaded colour and his masterly sense of design combine with a sense of humour which is both fiercely grotesque and refreshingly light-hearted. His anthropomorphic forms are, in a sense, cosmic and transcendental, yet they move and dance with the abandon of Walpurgis Night. Nothing of the intensity of earlier, more detailed, easel painting is lost in the precision and economy with which the murals are executed.

However, it was in sculpture and ceramics that Miró found the means to associate his work most closely with architecture, and, in consequence, to involve the public. The two great walls for the UNESCO building in Paris, which he completed with Artigas in 1957, the *Mural of the Moon* and the *Mural of the Sun*, are again designs of great intensity in which the technical

119

120, 121

120 TOP Joan Miró and Josep Llorens Artigas, *Mural of the Moon*, 1957
121 ABOVE Joan Miró and Josep Llorens Artigas, *Mural of the Sun*, 1957

hazards of the art of ceramics have been skilfully overcome.
Miró tells us: 'in spite of the precautions that can be taken,
the master of the work in the last resort is the fire; its action is
unpredictable and its sanction formidable. It is that that gives
this means of expression its value.'[3]

The ceramic design that Miró made in 1960 to replace the
painted mural at Harvard University proved once more that
his talent, combined with the technical skill of Artigas, could
produce very impressive murals. The monumental ceramic
for the façade of Terminal 2 at Barcelona airport, fifty metres
long by ten high, would eventually give Miró the scope and the
situation in a public place for which he had been preparing
himself for many years.

In the autumn of 1968 the citizens of Barcelona at last
acknowledged that they had a great artist among them. A
retrospective exhibition, showing every category of his work,
was held in the great halls of the ancient Hospital de la Santa
Cruz. In these surroundings the strength of his most recent
work found a natural affinity with the bold simplicity of
Catalan Gothic architecture. In the same year, the municipality

133

commissioned two more monumental works in addition to the mural for the airport. A sculpture sixty metres high, sited in the Parque Cervantes, would dominate the entrance into Barcelona by the main road from Madrid, while on the Ramblas, which lead from the harbour into the centre of the old city, Miró was asked to design a pavement. His work in three different manners thus dominates the three approaches – by air, by road and by sea – into his native city.

However, an even more impressive group of Miró sculptures and ceramics on a monumental scale was carefully planned by Miró at the Fondation Maeght at Saint-Paul de Vence in the south of France. The terraces that mount the hillside, close to galleries designed by José Luis Sert, form a labyrinth richly ornamented by Miró in a variety of ways. The siting of each piece was planned so that it plays its role in relation

122 *Moon, Sun and a Star: Project for a Monument to Barcelona*, 1967/cast 1969

123 *The Arch*, 1963

to the other sculptures and ceramics among the terraces
and the white walls of the buildings. Miró used water, pine
trees, terrace walls and the distant panorama of mountains
and the sea with great skill. His early admiration for Gaudí's
use of natural forms as an integral part of architecture, and
the pinnacles and terraces of Gaudí's Parque Güell, richly
encrusted with mosaic, influenced Miró in the dramatic use
of nature he made in the placing of his own sculpture.

    Many of the sculptures, now monumental in size, were first
conceived on a small scale. There are, for instance, a number
of diminutive variants of *The Arch* (1963) which dominates the
upper terraces of the Fondation Maeght. In the final work,
some adjustments in the proportions and a completely new

123

124 *The Pitchfork*, 1963

treatment of surface textures give it the authority of a unique
conception thoroughly integrated with its surroundings. From
a small plaster model, this has grown into a colossal triumphal
arch of biomorphic formation, with allusions to the anatomy
of women and birds. It is built in cement, but has occasional
incrustations of stone. Before it solidified, Miró incised
drawings of stars and other signs which endow its surface
with an intimate and decorative significance. The weathering
which takes place was accepted by Miró as an ally, even to the
welcome assistance of birds that nest in a dark hole in its flank.

124   There is another tall sculpture, *The Pitchfork* (1963), placed on
a terrace wall with a vast panorama as its background. In this
Miró was able to induce that marriage between empty space

and solid form which was to him a conception of fundamental importance. The construction, in bronze, is composed of three elements. It has a tall, slim body, the surface of which has been enriched with rough patches, as though handfuls of mud had been thrown at its even surface to convince us of its solidity. Above this rises a flat three-sided piece of bronze, in the centre of which a large circle has been cut as a window to the sky. Both these pieces are balanced at their base on curved surfaces, but the pitchfork, which crowns the headpiece like a plume, is even more surprising in its equilibrium. Placed as though on the tip of a vertical arrow it holds the sky in its prongs. The form is no more than a greatly enlarged replica of a Spanish peasant's pitchfork, but in this lofty position it appears to fly into the wind high over the valley like a bird.

Miró enjoyed the game of capturing space in a variety of ways. This element, in essence intangible and empty, can be given significance by becoming a sort of magnetic field between objects, or between hands or arms so placed that they control its presence. Miró could, in this way, make something out of nothing. He put empty space into a cage, or he could give it life as children do, as an invisible head behind a mask with holes cut out for eyes, nose and mouth. He took every advantage of the fact that our atmospheric space on earth, superior to space on the moon or elsewhere, is filled with air and impregnated with the germs of life. The seashell abandoned by its inmate can still vibrate with sound. A cave, or any gaping orifice, can fittingly suggest the presence of a voice; and the wind can actually invent its own melodies as it plays in the holes and hollows of the great sculptures set up on the terraces of Saint-Paul de Vence.

There is no more evocative trap for catching space than a circular hole such as that in the triangular head of *The Pitchfork*. Wherever it occurs, although essentially no more than a void, the empty circle becomes filled with associations that vary according to its position either as a source of light or as darkness. It may equally well be an eye, a mouth, the sun, an empty bottomless well or the crater of a volcano. Its ambiguity is matched by that of concave and convex surfaces: the convex surface of an eggshell encloses emptiness or the swelling germination of life; but by adding atmospheric colour and signs of movement Miró could give it the transparent depth of the sky before dawn. At Saint-Paul de Vence he set up a large ceramic, ovoid in shape, so that its dark reflection, mirrored in a pool of water, creates a splendid symbol of the all-enveloping and life-giving mystery of earth, air, water – and even fire, which, in this case, was an element essential to its formation.

125 Plate from *Album 13*, 1948

Graphics

It was not until 1930, ten years after Miró had become known as a painter, and had developed a highly personal style, that he made his first lithograph; his first etching came two years later. As time passed he showed an increasing interest in graphic art, and his eventual production was so prodigious that there was only one painter in his lifetime, Picasso, who surpassed him in the quantity of his output.

There were several reasons for his growing enthusiasm. The most obvious was the natural ease with which Miró's hand flowed across the paper. The exuberant enjoyment he found even in signing his own name with a thousand different flourishes, and the majestic handling of any ornament he might feel inclined to add, made him a great performer in the art of making signs. Much of this gift came probably from a natural talent characteristic of the Spanish, the origins of which are to be found in the caves of Altamira. In more recent times it has become a continuous tradition, in the Catalan 'primitives' and in folk art.

In addition there are the many different processes in engraving and lithography which offer scope for inventions

Sculpture and Other Media

126 *Small Engraving,* 1953

produced by unconventional means and new procedures. These again allowed Miró to take advantage of unexpected effects, chance happenings and even mistakes.

125, 126   Graphic art also appealed to Miró's desire to make his work less exclusive, and to overcome the formal limitations of the frame that an easel picture requires. It has the advantage of being less concentrated and more decorative, therefore more popular in its appeal. By offering the public the possibility of bypassing the museum and the exclusivity of the unique work of art, it belongs more widely to the community. Also, its production is often a matter of teamwork among artists and trained craftsmen. This introduces an element of anonymity, which was important to Miró, as it is to many artists.

Whatever technique Miró employed, lithography, etching, drypoint or woodcut, the result is one of extraordinary freshness. There is a brilliance in colour and variety of texture which arises from his sensibility towards the material on which the print is made, as well as the surface from which it is taken. Miró enjoyed making large prints on parchment or on a band of silk. He searched for paper of rare quality which could add a sensuous delight to the print, and mixed his techniques so as to preserve the dramatic surprise of the moment when the print separates, all fresh, from the plate.

There is a series of six large etchings of 1960, *The Giants*, which is typical of the strength of emotion that could be concentrated by Miró in a print. The spontaneity that he managed to capture in many of his later paintings is present here, with additional life and a magic violence that arises from the ultimate contact between the plate and the paper. The colours are as usual clear. They shine with significant precision through mists of random patterns in black and white. In spite of the poetic quality of his graphic work, Miró did not as a rule give titles to his prints himself; he relied on the sensibility of another poet, Jacques Dupin, to name them.

127
128

In the spring of 1969, with another burst of energy, Miró produced a remarkable series of engravings which
129
understandably he called 'monumental' on account of their size and the strength of their impact. He developed new processes in which a striking feature is the deeply embossed texture given to certain areas. The prints are astonishing in their vigour, and in the majestic assurance with which he was now able to integrate signs and symbols into three-dimensional designs. Contrasting the more liquid qualities of colour washes with fine lines engraved with precision, delicate nuances of flat surfaces with the turgid texture of embossed areas, vaporous depth with

127 *The Great Magician*, 1968

strong determined shapes in brilliant colour, he presented us with monumental engravings which have an intensity and a richness unparalleled in any former work.

During the same period he also worked on a series of lithographs which are equally successful. By using cloth printed with stripes or check patterns instead of paper, or making use of dress patterns as his ground, he managed to superimpose his compositions of figures and signs and arrive at results of an amazing variety. The variations on the original themes were accentuated by printing from the same stones in different colours, so that each print has a different appearance. It becomes evident when the prints in the series are spread out together that there can be no final solution. In Miró's hands each version has its own individual and convincing appeal.

The team of craftsmen who had helped in the printing of these graphics told me of the excitement they felt in working with Miró. After long periods of contemplation, he would plunge into new experiments, inventing unheard-of techniques with complete and unhesitating conviction. If, as sometimes happened, the results did not satisfy Miró, they were torn up at once and a new experiment began. The atmosphere was one of continuous exhilaration and youthful enthusiasm.

128 *In the Hail,* 1969

129 *The Calabash*, 1969

Miró's gift for calligraphy, and the ease with which
he played with colour, find a suitable outlet whenever he
designed a poster. The brilliance of the colour contrasts,
the unexpectedness of the layout and the flourish with which
his posters declare their purpose attract attention like a
trumpet call. When he made a book cover, an invitation card,
or whatever else he might have been asked to decorate, there
was always a similar conviction. There was strident authority
if it was to be sold for a good cause, like the silkscreen print
made in 1937, *Aidez l'Espagne*; there was an irresistible gaiety
if it was to be reproduced as a gift to his friends. Miró had an
unerring sense for the style, the colour, the material that the
occasion demanded.

68

It has been said of Miró that he was a 'painter's painter',
but he was also a musician's painter, and above all a poet's
painter. This made itself evident in his first lithographs,

Sculpture and Other Media

which were made in 1929–30 as illustrations to Tristan Tzara's poems *L'Arbre des voyageurs*. His desire to work in close association with his friends has resulted in an extraordinarily rich output of books of poems by them, decorated with unique ingenuity. Books such as Paul Eluard's *A Toute épreuve*, Tzara's *L'Antitête* and *Parler seul*, René Char's *A la santé du serpent*, Michel Leiris's *Bagatelles végétales*, René Crevel's *La Bague d'aurore*, Raymond Queneau's *Album 19* and Alfred Jarry's *Ubu Roi* are among Miró's most brilliant achievements.

130

But the originality and splendour of these books is matched by their rarity; they have of necessity been produced in a few limited editions and are less accessible than the numerous prints which Miró produced. One of his dramatic achievements in this category was the wartime *Barcelona Suite* of fifty lithographs. With the renewed possibility of travel after the war, Miró found that when abroad he could work more easily on graphic art than on painting, since it needed less continuous concentration. When he visited New York in 1947, he was invited by S. W. Hayter to use his studio and took the opportunity of experimenting in the new techniques in which Hayter was particularly proficient. Later, in Paris, the cooperation of experienced printers such as Lacourière, Mourlot and Crommelynck allowed Miró to realize his desire to work as the creative source among a team of highly qualified and sensitive craftsmen. Later, facilities offered to him at the Fondation Maeght encouraged Miró to produce some of the most brilliant graphic work of his whole career.

84

As the years passed, and Miró's activities multiplied, he systematically apportioned his time between Paris, where he had all the facilities and the expert assistance he needed for his graphic work, Gallifa, where Artigas prepared for his arrival with skill and devotion the raw material for his ceramics, the studios and workshops at Calamayor, and the remote farm at Montroig. Calamayor and Montroig were kept free for the solitary contemplation that accompanied Miró's painting, and the flashes of inspiration by which he pieced together and brought his sculpture to life.

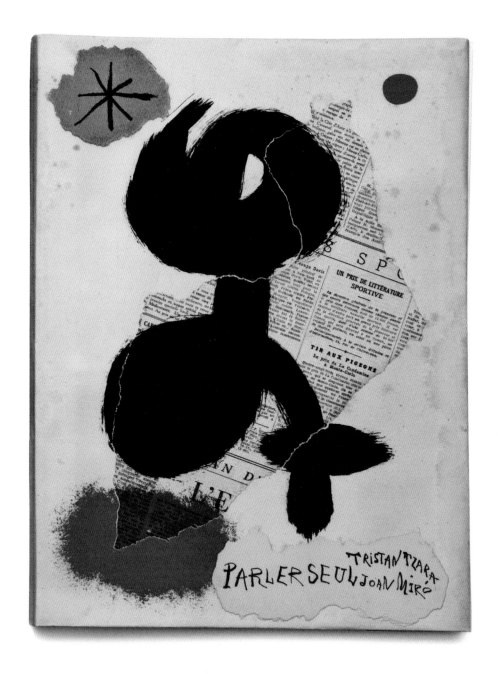

130 Cover for Tristan Tzara's *Parler seul*, 1948–50

Chapter 7
Poetry and Reality

Every artist must find in their work their own method of inducing their imagination to take shape, and to develop some initial idea, however trivial, into a work of art saturated with meaning. The idea, according to Miró, comes with the sensation of a shock, the intensity of which is sufficient to initiate a tension of spirit which leads to new emotional activity. He explained at some length how the process seems to take place. It is important, he insisted, that a great variety of incidents should be capable of bringing about this state of mind; but it should not be provoked by 'chemical means such as drink or drugs'. Also, it is unlikely that the same methods will act twice in the same way; if this happened it could lead to the formation of a system, and this would impair or destroy the spontaneity which is an essential element in this process. It is only through the uncharted channels of the subconscious that the main stream of inspiration can flow freely.

'I work better when I am not working than when I am', he told me, 'like Saint-Pol Roux who used to put a notice outside his door, LE POÈTE TRAVAILLE ["The Poet works"], when he intended to sleep.' But the tension that gives birth to ideas can also come through incidents and surprises which happen when the artist is wide awake, or during the long hours when they contemplate objects which may become particularly charged with interest.

Miró told Yvon Taillandier:

The atmosphere which favours this tension, I find in poetry, music, architecture – Gaudí, for example, is terrific – in my daily walks, in certain noises: the noise of horses in the country, the creaking of wooden cartwheels, footsteps, cries in the night, crickets. The spectacle of the sky overwhelms me.... Empty spaces, empty horizons, empty plains – everything that is bare has always greatly impressed me.[1]

164

But the atmosphere is productive only when it somehow provokes a deep, urgent reaction:

I work in a state of passion and compulsion. When I begin a canvas, I obey a physical impulse, a need to act; it's like a physical discharge.... I begin my pictures under the effect of a shock...which makes me escape from reality. The cause of this shock may be a tiny thread sticking out of the canvas, a drop of water falling, this print made by my finger on the shining surface of this table. In any case I need a point of departure, even if it's only a speck of dust or a flash of light. This form begets a series of things, one thing giving birth to another thing.

From the moment when the initial shock has set the imagination in motion another process follows. 'I have always felt that I am like an insect with antennae,' Miró told me. 'I hover and find myself directed mysteriously to further discoveries.' But once the contact between him and his work had been established, the discoveries came from chance happenings in the work itself. A continuous feedback took place from the work which had already gained a life of its own.

The process, however, was not necessarily continuous. In his studio Miró kept round him scores of canvases in all states of progress, some scarcely begun and others awaiting, possibly for years, the moment when that communion between him and his work would allow him to establish the final state of tension he wished it to contain. When this happened, there followed a feeling of detachment and a shift of interest from the finished work to younger, less developed members of the family that he was constantly bringing to life.

In spite of his distrust of all systems, Miró counted on certain sources on which he habitually relied for stimulation. In addition to chance happenings and the unlimited sources of nature, he kept round him a stock of objects, each containing some provocative significance, and images cut out from magazines and pinned to the wall, remarkable either for their fantasy or their banality. Between this raw material and the finished work, of which sometimes they may bodily become part, lay a path paved with hesitations and uncertainty. Stacks of canvases of all sizes, in varying states of preparation, and half-finished sculptures, waited round him like cultures in which the imagination can germinate. Meanwhile, they were still at work in Miró's mind, although dormant for an unpredictable time.

Occasionally, a blank canvas received the first traces, sketched lightly in charcoal, of an idea which would perhaps be left for months to develop until the moment came when Miró felt clearly the exact shape of the dominant lines and the colour that would be their accompaniment. Or it might be that, when finishing work for the day, Miró would wipe his palette-knife, his hands or even his feet on a new canvas, leaving a pattern of coloured blobs, stains or footprints on its surface. Accidents such as these were essential opening gambits which provoked new trails of thought and opened unexpected doors to the imagination.

Miró's observation was not necessarily confined to chance or to nature, although these provided unlimited resources. 44, 45 Just as he found his inspiration for the *Dutch Interiors* in the seventeenth-century paintings in the museums of Holland, he might find a sudden interest in the banality and false values of a commercial reproduction and proceed to transform it by adding to its surface the vigorous signs that emerged from the fleeting reality of his dreams; or he would select a thoroughly insincere and trivial landscape painted by an obscure artist and, in reaction to its vulgarity, he would joyously paint it over with a strong rhythm of black lines and flat colours. The result was a new and fantastic reality that forms a strange marriage between inadequate representation and powerful poetic symbolism.

In a different mood, Miró took as his point of departure 131 a landscape of Château-Thierry by Camille Corot in which a

131 Camille Corot, *Château-Thierry, General View without the Tower of St-Crépin*, 1856 or 1863

132 *Homage to Corot*, 1967

small accent of colour, the red hat of a figure seated by a river, gives meaning to the sensitive greens, greys and ochres of the whole composition. There were three factors in the Corot that triggered off Miró's enthusiasm and resulted in a large canvas,
132   *Homage to Corot* (1967). The first was the piquant economy in the touch of bright red, the second the shape of a clump of trees surrounding a house in the middle distance, and the third the grey sky. The foreground shadow he characteristically transformed into impenetrable blackness. Otherwise the complete liberty with which Miró set to work removed his version so far from the original source of inspiration that it is only by the title that the connection still remains.

Miró's way of finding another point of departure in collage is well illustrated by the way in which he derived the series of
53-56   great paintings of 1933 from the catalogue of a hardware store. It was often been in the annihilation of literal images and their translation into poetic signs that Miró enjoyed a sense of elation and freedom, but not infrequently an image banal or sentimental in itself was allowed to play its part intact. Its incongruous presence brings a reference to the reality of our

133 Maquette for Barcelona airport mural, 1968–69

daily preoccupations in sharp contrast with the fantasy of the surrounding forms.

Miró's capacity to utilize borrowed images and recognizable objects went beyond two-dimensional art. He found a wide field for the transformation of objects into sculptures which contain new, often grotesque, personalities. He collected a great variety of derelict objects which intrigued him by some hidden significance. As his friend Prats says: 'When I pick up a stone, it's a stone. When Miró picks up a stone, it's a Miró.'[2] The corners of his studios were crowded with rusty pieces of iron, twisted wires, bones, broken electric bells, horns, old roots, stones, pots, peasants' tools and pieces of tinsel. I have watched him try out various combinations and suddenly, seeing a solution that fascinated him, build up from pieces of scrap a figure with a strangely convincing personality – a chimera, benign or evil in character, but essentially humorous. Unexpected encounters between objects such as he brought about are always humorous, and yet are also part of the solemn magic game at which Miró was an adept.

In spite of Miró's method of working on many paintings and sculptures concurrently over a long period, there is a consistency in each work, due to the patience with which he waited for the moment when the material spoke to him and revealed the means by which he could bring it fully to life. Accidents and the shock that accompanies them are the most unfailing means of creating that tension of the spirit which he recognized as being essential. 'I work like a gardener or a vinedresser,' he told Yvon Taillandier. 'Things come slowly. My vocabulary of forms, for example – I didn't discover it all

109–11

at once. It formed itself almost in spite of me. Things follow
their natural course. They grow, they ripen. I must graft. I must
water, as with lettuces. Ripening goes on in my mind. So I'm
always working on a great many things at the same time.'[3]

There were days of taking in, of absorbing sensations, just
as there were days of giving out, and it was Miró's patience and
the solitary concentration of his whole sensibility that rewarded
him with a spontaneous and vigorous renewal of his inspiration.
'Every day I risk my neck,' he repeated to me, categorically.

There are, however, demands which call for a method which
cannot be left entirely to spontaneity. On several occasions Miró
accepted a commission for a monumental work and operated in
a more calculated way. When he was asked to execute the vast
mural at the airport of Barcelona, his first step was to spend,
alone on the site, several days and sleepless nights. It was the
absence of a conversation with a work already taking shape
that made the task much harder, since he must not allow his
finished calculations to overwhelm the element of spontaneity.
Finally, when he began to work on a maquette laid out on the
floor of his studio, it was completed in bold outline and brilliant
primary colours in the space of half an hour. The result was
powerful and definitive, and Miró was satisfied not only by the
admirable simplicity of his solution but also by the knowledge
that the process of translating the maquette into a ceramic fifty
metres long by ten metres high, on which he would collaborate
with his friend Artigas, would inevitably reintroduce an element
of chance. In the firing of the hundreds of tiles required, slight
variations in colour and texture would again bring unexpected
detail and the incalculable presence of life.

Poetry and Reality

Titles

134

The lark's wing encircled with golden blue rejoins the heart of the poppy sleeping on the diamond-studded meadow: this is the title of a large painting of 1967 which appears at first to be an abstract composition. But Miró tells us that although he never started a painting from a given title he often discovered a title, more or less elaborate, at an early stage. 'I find my titles gradually as I work, as I link one thing to another on my canvas. When I've found the title I live in its atmosphere. The title then becomes a hundred per cent reality for me, like a model – a reclining woman, say – for someone else. For me the title is an exact reality.'[4] This unusual process, in which a painting becomes linked with, and in some ways dependent on, a poetic idea, should be understood if we are to enjoy Miró's work to the full.

If we look again at the painting I have just mentioned, bearing in mind its title, new elements come into play. The lark's wing has acquired a blue aura from the sky, and we now realize that we are enveloped in golden light, looking down from a height at a small scarlet poppy which illuminates the space round it like the sparkle of diamonds. The title becomes a poetic accompaniment to the painting and also supplies an interpretation of colour and space that extends and completes their effect.

What follows is more than an eyeful of colour. Our vision is accompanied by a giddiness when we realize we are no longer on the earth but enjoying the exhilaration of the lark, detached, looking down and astonished at the brilliance of one small red flower in a great expanse of green grass. Instead of offering purely abstract visual pleasures, title and painting now create together new metaphors for space, movement and the life of the fields.

There are many other instances in which the title provides a new element when read with the picture, but in some cases the title is incorporated into the painting itself. In *Le corps de ma brune...* (1925), the inscription covers the whole canvas in such a way that the words play a major part in the composition, a method also used by Max Ernst. In a later painting of 1968 the stencilled letters of the word 'silence' are scattered over a large red patch in the centre in such a way that as we read them the repetition of the 'E' seems to evoke distant echoes – echoes that are taken up by other signs that we find repeated with diminishing size into the distance. It is as though we had shouted SILE–E–E–NCE within some vast echoing hall, and it is typical of the reversals of positive and negative that Miró so often used that silence should be the means of creating sound.

38
135

134 *The lark's wing encircled with golden blue rejoins the heart of the poppy sleeping on the diamond-studded meadow, 1967*

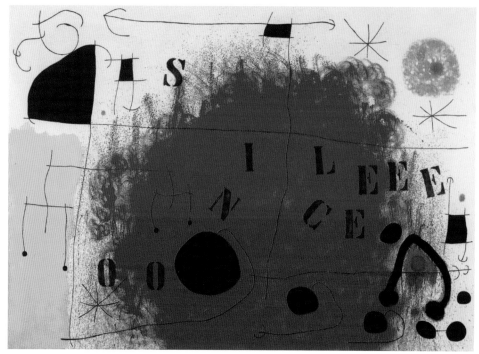

135 *Silence*, 1968

But although Miró was highly sensitive to music, and gave titles to his paintings such as *Dancer Listening to the Organ in a Gothic Cathedral* or *Woman Listening to Music*, he realized that any reference to sound in painting is bound to be ambiguous. He always worked in complete silence, but the influence of music can be felt in his painting in the vibration of lines or colours. In the painting entitled *Silence*, he arrived at a more literal metaphor.

In modern art the title was often condemned as a literary impurity unnecessary for the appreciation of the visual arts. Abstract painters such as Mondrian preferred to number their works or use the title merely as a means of identification. Traditionally the title has been little more than a description of the content of the painting, with some notable exceptions such as Goya's titles for his series of etchings *Los Caprichos* (1797–99), which were intended to extend the allegorical element.

The surrealists deliberately began to override the barriers between poetry and painting, and chose to do so in ways which were ambiguous and calculated to provoke the imagination by their incongruity. However, in his early work, during the period

172   Chapter 7

of his closest association with the surrealists, Miró took little interest in titles. Like Picasso, he found that a painting can speak for itself, though in some cases a title asserted itself or was invented by his friends. It was about 1930 that titles, apart from those written on the canvas as part of the composition, began to become a feature of importance in his work.

Owing to the way in which his working process developed, in his later works the title emerged out of the unfinished painting; it became, as he said, his model – an invisible idea takes visual form. This reaction between different but inseparable kinds of imagery enriched his work with surprising and unorthodox metaphors. A list of his titles could be enjoyed as a poem; but this is not their purpose. They are accompaniments intended to intensify the lyrical atmosphere, or subtly to extend the dimensions of the work, and as such they should always be read attentively as part of the picture.

The Night

If we should wish to select one theme which dominates the work of Miró more than any other, the night could, for many reasons, be chosen and made his emblem. This is the coat of arms in which Miró most readily clothed himself, and by which we can identify and recognize the dominant characteristics of his power to captivate us.

In the 1920s Miró had found a generous source of inspiration in that phenomenon of the night, the dream, and had transposed the immeasurable influences which stir in the subconscious into the conscious realm of our waking hours. His friends, the surrealist poets and painters, discovered in him an Orpheus who could go into the underworld of night and, unscathed, bring out mysterious signs – who could give evidence of the indissoluble links between the world in which we move and are conscious, and that unknown world which none the less envelops and influences us – who could bring together the luminous world of day and the sombre realm of night.

This does not imply that Miró was obsessed with obscurity and darkness. He was far too conscious of the light and the vital colour of the world in which we live. It was his appreciation of the contrast between night and day that raised him to a unique position – his consciousness that the night, which can present itself as the symbol of death, is also the womb of creation, that grass grows by night, and that, strangely enough, physically we can see further by night than by day, for by night the stars, chosen by Miró as his most persistent symbol, can appear to be close at hand, while by day they are invisible.

While the light of day reassures us of the identity of the world around us, night is rich in ambiguities and confusions that upset our confidence. On the one hand we can find solace in the silent calm of night: we are warmed by the embrace of love and the confidence of sleep; we rejoice in the fecundity peculiar to the hours of darkness, the time of conception and of growth, and in the visions to which night gives birth in the imagination. Yet, beside all these delights, there lurks the terror engendered by the night, isolation, blindness, the nightmare, the demons of uncertainty and the semblance of death.

Darkness can surround us like the walls of a prison, and yet the prisoner waits for night to make his escape. Night closes in on us, and yet space becomes more vast and limitless around us. Our sense of distance becomes unsettled. Dwarves become giants, and our normal sense of measures and proportions suffers bewildering distortions. Time also changes its rhythm; the brief passage between sleeping and waking can seem endless in our dreams. But whether we are asleep or awake, the night carries with it a condition which is more primeval than the day. Our sensations are closer to the source of consciousness, to primitive fears, hopes and memories, than the rational control of our waking hours will permit.

Miró appreciated the value of the night, above all for the spiritual freedom that it offers, and for the ambiguities and contrasts it implies. The escape it affords from the tyranny of everyday affairs, and the vision that rewards us when only the eye of the imagination is active, become apparent in the manner in which he interpreted his inspiration. He gave substance to visions that have their source in the subconscious – visions that are most vivid when the liberating influences of sleep and the night envelop us in a solitary trance.

His love of the unattainable, his mystic marriages with the stars, are passionate and enduring emotions, but the medium he used was visual, finite and more direct in its appeal. In our time the solitary transcendental love of the mystic has become a rarity; the dark night of the soul is disturbed by the glare of modern technical discoveries. Miró was essentially modern. His sensibility extended from the primeval magic of the cave paintings to the banalities of factory-made objects. It is understandable that for him and for us, the dark night should now be illuminated with brilliant colour and the clash of contradictory ideas. The night of Miró reflects the realities of the modern age.

Nor did Miró necessarily think of the night in subtle metaphysical metaphors. As an untiring observer he says: 'I'm overwhelmed when I see, in an immense sky, the crescent of the moon, or the sun,' and adds: 'In the contemporary visual climate, I like factories, nocturnal lights, the world seen from a 'plane. I owe one of the greatest emotions of my life to a night flight over Washington. Seen from a 'plane a city is a marvellous thing.'[5]

A glance at the titles that form accompaniments to Miró's paintings will convince us of his interest and give us clues to those things associated with the night that enchant him most. There are mysterious nocturnal happenings (*A drop of dew, falling from the wing of a bird, wakes Rosalie, asleep in the shadow of a spider's web*); amorous encounters (*Numbers and constellations in love with a woman*); magic influences (*People, magnetized by the stars walking on the music of a furrowed landscape*); secret intimacies (*Woman with a blonde armpit dressing her hair by the light of the stars*); romantic tenderness (*The nightingale's song at midnight and morning rain* and *By moonlight the setting sun caresses us*); allusions to the return of the light (*The mauve of the moon covers the green of the frog on the departure of darkness*, *Hope Comes Back to Us as the Constellations Flee*, and *The Blaze of the Sun Wounds the Lingering Star*).

Above all the presence of woman dominates Miró's night. There are *Women and Kites among the Stars*, *Women and Little Girls Skipping by Night* and *Women with Dishevelled Hair Welcoming the Crescent of the Moon*. There are rites celebrating the presence of woman throughout the night: *Birds and Shooting Stars Encircling a Woman in the Night* and *Woman Hypnotized by Rays of Twilight Stroking the Plain*, and a number of paintings entitled *Women and Bird in Front of the Moon*.

Often the presence of a woman is accompanied by the 'bird of night', not infrequently in close association with flight from the constraints of day: *The Star Rises, the Birds Fly Away, People Dance* – while elsewhere there is a *Woman Dreaming of Escape* and, near by, *The Ladder of Escape* and *The Passage of the Divine Bird*, or, again, *The Wings of the Bird Slide Over the Moon to Reach the Stars*.

Such titles in themselves give insight into the tenderness and the alarm with which Miró examined nocturnal activity. From twilight to dawn, the night becomes a stage, set for a strange cosmic drama in which creatures of the night, the snail, the bird of night, the frog, the spider, exchange places with the stars and the moon in a festive celebration of woman: *A Star Caresses the Breast of a Negress*. There is a nocturnal indifference to the recognized magnitude of all things. The boundless space that first appears in the early 'dream paintings' confirms the sensation that the night accentuates a consciousness of the infinity of space and that darkness, far from being merely the negation of light, contains every imaginable colour. Miró's night skies are often white, and the stars, the moon, even the sun, become black or laden with colour.

Although this preoccupation with the night is more obom obvious in paintings since the *Constellations* of 1940–41, we find deliberate reference to the allegory of night and day in 23 *The Farm* as early as 1921–22, where the immaculate disc of the sun, set in an immense blue sky, finds its echo in the black circular shadow in the earth at the foot of the tree. In this bond between positive and negative polarities the great tree finds the direction of its growth from darkness to light. In 42 other paintings, such as *Dog Barking at the Moon* (1926), Miró treats the night as an observed phenomenon rather than as an atmosphere in which we become immersed, and we find here an early appearance of that symbol that later recurs so often, the ladder of escape which leads deep into the solitude of night. But it was in the 'dream paintings' of 1925 onwards that a new preoccupation with night began to develop. Limitless space, inherent in darkness, and the atmosphere of sleep found a new emphasis in his work. Dreams and hallucinations – influences contrary to the hard facts of daily life, but emanating from the subconscious – entered into his painting with the freshness of dew. The vast empty spaces he created, detached from all reference to earth or the horizon, became populated with shapes related to the phantoms that appear in states of half-consciousness.

As the political atmosphere darkened, and Miró's painting became prophetic of approaching catastrophes, he found 53, 54 in the great compositions of 1933 the means of enveloping the spectator in an atmosphere of primeval night. We are led into vast caves inhabited by magic animals, a twilight in which creatures of darkness float and dance, not on the ground but among the stars. His disquiet increased and 62 made itself felt dramatically in his *peintures sauvages*, in which the skies behind grotesque figures of men, women and monsters become opaque with the blackness of a sinister and artificial night. The turbulent darkness that was descending 66 culminated in the *Still-life with Old Shoe* (1937), that powerful allegory of civil war. With great eloquence, Miró used black as 71 a colour in several paintings such as *Head of a Woman* (1938), in which the image of woman suffered cruel metamorphoses, appearing as a monster of the night, black and yet adorned with the brilliant regalia of her attributes.

136 *Nocturne*, 1938

The night in its many aspects is not, however, in itself evil. It is capable of harbouring, even during Miró's most heart-breaking years, an assembly of gay and scintillating creatures presided over by a star, as in *Nocturne* (1938).

136

During the first tragic weeks of the Nazi invasion of France, it was in this more lyrical mood that he produced that very beautiful and poetic series of small paintings, the *Constellations*, which are fundamentally an ode to the night from twilight to dawn, an ode to its population of nocturnal creatures, the dew, the nightingale, the stars. Talking of this a few years later, he said: 'I felt a profound desire to escape. I deliberately withdrew into myself. The night, music, the stars, began to play a major part in suggestions for my pictures.' Throughout this brilliant series, woman is supreme, encircled by her lovers, creatures of darkness, the birds, the stars.

78–82

In the paintings that follow, like *Women and Bird in Front of the Moon* (1944), night is no longer dominated by the evil obscurity of war and terror. It has borrowed from the dawn the

137

137 *Women and Bird in Front of the Moon*, 1944

colour of courage; people dance, once more refreshed by the coolness of the night. With the power of a magician, Miró fills the night sky with light, knowing that the night is not blind, that we can see in darkness, and that, on the contrary, it is the light that can blind us. Miró sees by night, his darkness is flooded with colour and infinite in its space. In a painting of 1953 a sun, black as night, appears beside a dark star. In a masterly way he succeeds in revealing to us a conception of space that unites the dichotomy of night and day.

99 The three large canvases of 1961, *Blue I, II, III*, illustrate this unity very beautifully; but no painting can convince us better than the later works of 1968 which appear to be an ultimate refinement of this same theme. They were first shown, most appropriately, on three walls of a small Gothic chapel. The title given by Miró to the paintings in this triptych is *Painting on White Background for the Cell of a Recluse*. Each of the great canvases has no more than a single tenuous black line that crosses its immaculate whiteness, and in each case this happens with a different motion. To follow its course inch by inch is to accompany a determined explorer crossing a vast, empty but luminous space. If, however, we imagine this seen in negative, we have a white line moving across a totally black sky, like a flash of lightning. But Miró's version, the negative of the storm by night, is even more dramatic and more stimulating to the imagination – it is the triumph of light over darkness.

138 Among Miró's later sculptures there are two large pieces
139 of 1966 which evoke the theme of day and night: *Solar Bird* and *Lunar Bird*. Both these works exist in two versions, one in bronze and the other in pure white marble. Here the darkness of the bronze version, with its star-like reflections of light, is more evocative of the roles that Miró attributes to these two astral bodies.

Of the two figures, 'ageless toys astonished to see themselves suddenly promoted to the dignity of idols',[6] the sun bird, surprisingly, is considerably the smaller but clearly contains a greater degree of energy. His movement is horizontal and of great vigour, driven from the rear as though by jet propulsion. He appears to be eternally active, busy like a man determined never to be late in his daily round of appointments; practical and steadfast, he carries on his back a crescent moon.

In contrast the moon bird is wayward and variable, a bird without wings. She seems more firmly attached to the soil and is dominated by an upward growth which culminates in two great horns that sprout from the ripening crescent of her head. Always, whether she is causing the dog to bark, presiding over woman, making the ocean pulsate or being bleached out by the dawn, Miró attributes to the moon a greater mystery than to her companion the sun, more monotonous in his habits. Queen of the night, she rules mysteriously; her influences are disconcerting, her course erratic. Yet all female creatures obey her, and in the realm of dreams she is supreme.

It is commonly known that all cats are black at night, and this knowledge might encourage us to think that Miró loved the night for its anonymity. He tells us:

We must move towards anonymity. Today we are more and more aware of the need of it. But at the same time we are aware of the need for an absolutely individual gesture, completely anarchic from the social point of view. Why? Because a profoundly individual gesture is anonymous. Being anonymous, it allows the universal to be attained, I feel sure: the more local anything is, the more universal.[7]

In these words Miró expresses the union between solitude and universality that can be felt above all at night. But this brief examination of his work should be sufficient to convince us that for him the night did not envelop everything in a formless, colourless, intangible haze; on the contrary, he knew the varied characteristics of the inhabitants of night intimately, their explosive brilliance and the absorbent depth of their shadows. Among the many enchantments revealed to us by his genius he showed us the thousand eyes and the multitude of wonders hidden in the immeasurable scope of night, that short passage between the light of two successive days which nevertheless occupies a very large part of our lives. In the words of an ancient Hindu sage:

That which for all men is the night,
In that, the poet is awake.
And in that in which all men are awake,
That is the night for the poet.

The Ladder of Escape
The ladder, that simple device which allows us to rise above the earth, gather fruit or hide away in the branches of a tree, made its first appearance in Miró's paintings in *The Farm* (1921–22). Beginning with its literal representation in this picture, the ladder was soon endowed with a wider significance. In *Carnival of Harlequin* (1924–25) it leads us with its tapering perspective into regions of fantasy where elegant creatures shaped like mermaids float out from between the rungs.

23

26

138 TOP *Solar Bird*, 1966
139 RIGHT *Lunar Bird*, 1966

In *Dog Barking at the Moon* (1926), the ladder leads out into an empty sky, while in many other paintings such as *A Star Caresses the Breast of a Negress* (1938) it has become a purely schematic sign which penetrates into the unknown. Its shape is made to imply movement, an invitation to follow the direction in which it points, to rise beyond the limitations that bind us to earth, to escape from the material world into the realms of the spirit. The symbol was used persistently by Miró because of its power to describe graphically his own desire to transcend the incomplete condition of daily life.

In earlier years Miró's close contact with surrealism had already convinced him that art, if it exists at all, implies something more than the enjoyment of beauty. His investigation of the world of dreams and the subconscious was made with the desire to approach, to use Herbert Read's term, 'the frontiers of perception', regardless of the risks involved. There was never any doubt in his mind that what was of real importance to him lay beyond painting. The degree of sheer visual pleasure that paintings give can be intense; but the more acute it becomes the more it is likely to provoke a further yearning, often ill-defined but of great strength, for a transcendental understanding of our condition. The work of art then, as it leads us to the frontiers of perception, becomes the medium which can give access to new states of consciousness. In itself, though it remains the motive force, it becomes less important than the state of mind to which it leads. At the same time the artist themself also recedes into a condition of anonymity. 'Anonymity', Miró says, 'allows me to renounce myself but in renouncing myself I come to affirm myself more strongly.... The same practice makes me seek the noise hidden in silence, the movement in immobility, life in the inanimate, the infinite in the finite, forms in space and myself in anonymity.'[8] Artists such as Miró, who have discovered through paradox that the finite statement of their work can be a gateway to a new perception of the infinite rather than an end in itself, accept the role of prophet, or rather seer. They become the intermediaries who, instinctively in the first place and later by their command of aids and techniques, can carry us with them into a more complete understanding of our human relationship to the great unknown, towards an accord between us and the nature of all things.

Hindu philosophy tells us that 'he who understands has wings'. The idea of flight as a symbol of liberation is widespread. It is tempting to find a similarity between the atmosphere created by Miró and shamanic rites in which the adept is able to visit the celestial paradise and describe to their audience in detail all they see and all that happens. The importance of this is the primitive conception that it is necessary for the seer not only to see beyond our usual limits and restore to their audience contact with the transcendental, but also to perfect their means of doing so. Such means of entering into a state of ecstasy will inevitably involve symbols and metaphors. The shaman takes imaginary wings, mounts from the earth by means of a tree or a liana, or, as in Siberia, climbs up a post in the middle of the tent and out by the smoke-hole. 'But', according to the religious scholar Mircea Eliade, 'we know that this opening, made to let out smoke, is likened to the "hole" made by the pole-star in the vault of Heaven'[9] – an elementary but vivid metaphorical description of the transcendental process.

These yearnings arise, wherever they occur, from the necessity for a liberation from the bonds of the material world; a universal means of attaining this transcendence is found in the use of symbols born from a state of trance. The universality of the symbols implies that they belong to the collective unconscious. They are the product of a trance state which resembles the paradisaic condition attained by the shaman through their rites. For the shaman 'sacred stones or trees', to quote Eliade, 'are not adored in their natural capacity, but only because they are *hierophanies*, because they "show forth" something which is no longer mineral or vegetable but sacred – "wholly other".'[10]

We can recognize in this primitive conception Miró's belief in the necessity for metamorphosis, an idea which dominates also the writings of Antonin Artaud whom Miró remembered as one of the most important influences in his early friendship with the surrealists. In his book *Héliogabale*, Artaud pursues this ancient belief:

I mean to say that in Syria the earth lives and that there are stones that live.... There are black stones in the form of the penis of a man with a woman's sex chiselled below. Such stones are the vertebrae in the precious corners of the earth.... But there are stones that live as plants and animals live, and as it may be said the sun lives.[11]

The daemonic writings of Artaud were accepted by Miró in a manner that worked deeply on his imagination. Ideas born from them continued to appear in his work years later, as for instance in the great ceramic *Woman and Bird* (1962), which has embedded in its upright phallic shape a bold symbolic representation of the vulva. This is not a literal illustration of the black stones mentioned by Artaud; it is significant as a sign

140

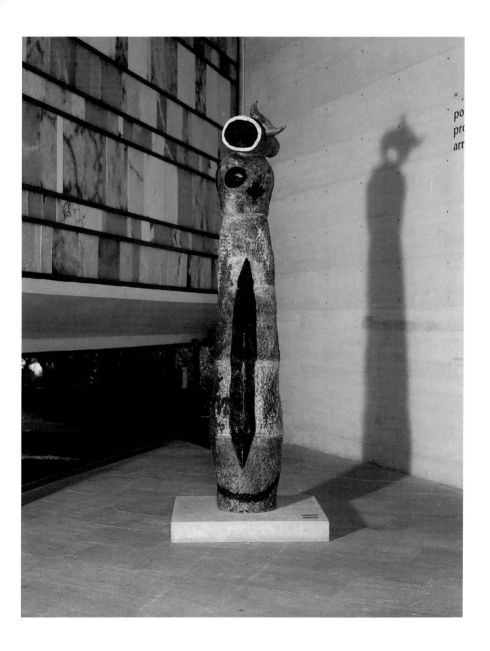

140 Joan Miró and Josep Llorens Artigas, *Woman and Bird*, 1962

of the animistic conception of the world which Miró shared with his friend. 'It is the spirit of a stone that acts. The stone itself is without value,' he told me, and went on to describe his last visit to Artaud when his friend was a mental patient at the Hôpital Sainte-Anne in Paris. Artaud, who was then a very sick man, seized an axe in the hospital garden and with terrifying cries began to cut down a tree which to him had become an embodiment of evil; this scene troubled Miró profoundly. An act of such frenzied violence was completely foreign to his nature, but he recognized at its source the same animism which he shared with the poet.

The vestiges of primitive understanding that we inherit in myth are all inseparable from an element of mystery – a form of understanding which convinces us but cannot be explained logically. Miró often expressed a great admiration for the poetry of Stéphane Mallarmé. The work to which he felt most closely akin is that unprecedented and enigmatic poem 'Un coup de dés jamais n'abolira le hasard', in which the poet scatters lines and words across the page, taking into account the visual importance of the white spaces between them. In his preface to the poem Mallarmé says: 'The paper intervenes each time an image ceases or enters of its own accord.'[12] The last lines of the poem express a conviction of the intrinsic value of doubt, meditation and chance:

veillant
doutant
roulant
brillant et méditant
avant de s'arrêter
à quelque point dernier qui le sacre
Toute Pensée émet un Coup de Dés

('...watching/doubting/wandering/shining and meditating/ before coming to a stop/at some final point that consecrates it/ Every Thought emits a Casting of the Dice')

Like Mallarmé, Miró knew that we see furthest when we perceive things as though through a veil which cannot be lifted entirely and by which the imagination is nourished and made active. At the poetic level we see and we interpret, but must never destroy what we have seen and felt by saying too much. There is a region, midway between the disintegration of chaos and the sterility of infallible order, in which life exists. It is at this precarious level that Miró opens our eyes and provides access to new regions. He does not propose that we should struggle to attain either hell or heaven, but rather to gain a truer understanding of their coexistence and our own relationship to both extremes. Miró shows us at every turn that it is not the sublime that leads to the transcendental; the reality of material things can provide the starting point for our voyage of escape – a voyage which is essentially creative and valid as an experience, because it is spiritually and materially the ultimate symbol of life. R. D. Laing, approaching this conception from the point of view of the psychiatrist, says: 'Man, most fundamentally, is not engaged in the discovery of what is there, nor in production, nor even in communication, nor in invention. He is enabling being to emerge from non-being.'[13] Miró, in his early belief that art must emerge from anti-art, already recognized the existence of this fundamental truth. In its later developments his anti-art became the medium, the experience transcending himself, which can be shared by all.

Reality

Miró's evolution from an artist closely attached to peasant origins, seeking to represent nature with an almost pedestrian realism, to a seer whose aim is a transcendental escape, suggests paradoxically that there is a parallel between him and Mondrian, for whom he expressed such contempt in early days. In a letter written to me in later life, Miró explained his present attitude:

I have a profound respect for Mondrian. Although we are at opposite poles, he takes things to their limit and sacrifices everything to attain purity. He leaves the dramatic realism of his first period to arrive at this saintliness. His influence is widespread, but he should remain a unique case in the history of art. As for me, the more ignoble I find life, the more strongly I react by contradiction in humour and in an outburst of liberty and expansion.

It is here that we find once more the importance of contradictory elements to Miró himself; we recognize his love of paradox, and the stimulus he gained from adversity. Elsewhere, this painter who enchanted us so often by the brilliance of his humour confesses that by nature he is tragic and taciturn: 'I am a pessimist. I think that everything is going to turn out very badly. If there is anything humorous about my painting, it has not been consciously sought. This humour comes perhaps from the need I feel to escape from the tragic side of my temperament. It's a reaction, but an involuntary one.'[14]

The humour of Miró often has a flavour of violence, and frequently evokes a sense of cruelty which is highly disturbing. In that way it is essentially Spanish. His attack on the human image, both visual and conceptual, is devastating and fundamentally akin to the violent distortions of Picasso. But in a less violent mood the contortions and expressions of his figures provoke laughter by their innocent buffoonery; and laughter caused by the grotesque, Baudelaire tells us, 'has about it something profound, primitive and axiomatic, which is closer to the innocent life and to absolute joy than is the laughter caused by the comic in man's behaviour'.[15]

Humour is after all a means of lifting us from one plane to another, and offers a form of escape. Miró used it instinctively to lead us beyond the trivial, knowing that the universal fund of banality and triviality that surrounds us is the raw material from which he must draw. It is here that he never lost the peasant wisdom that he expressed by saying: 'it is essential to have your feet firmly planted on the soil in order to leap into the air.'

The paradoxical nature of Miró's attitude to the real is further illustrated in his artistic relationship with his great contemporary and compatriot, Picasso. Both artists felt a compulsion to question their own achievements; their careers illustrate the saying of Max Jacob, an early friend of them both: 'le doute, voilà l'art!' ('Doubt: that's art!').[16] The element of doubt which acts as a stimulus towards new achievements becomes a salutary torment from which it is impossible to escape. It eliminates the deadly possibility of self-satisfaction and sharpens perception and poetic insight.

While discussing some of his own paintings Picasso said: 'Like all Spaniards I am above all a realist.' His statement should, and in fact does, apply to Miró; but we know also that there are many different interpretations of reality, each allowing its interpreter to be called a realist.

A definition of the realism of Picasso is difficult because in the variety of his styles there is a disconcerting disparity between, for instance, his cubist paintings and the work of his neoclassical period, in which the method of representing form is more conventional. It is however always possible, even in his most hermetic style, to trace a relationship back to some objective observation. Picasso's imagery always originates in his acute and penetrating ability to observe the world around him, even though it may become surprisingly transformed in the process of creation.

The same approach to painting was inherent in Miró and is clearly visible up to the time when he painted *The Farm*, but

23

from then onwards he began to rely progressively on the reality of his dreams and the fecundity of an imagination which was constantly receiving nourishment both from the subconscious and the outside world. This approach led to a new sense of reality which transcended a literal representation of objects and found its expression in signs and symbols which attain a universal or archetypal meaning.

To illustrate the difference between these interpretations of reality we have only to look at the two murals, *Guernica* and *The Reaper*, painted by Picasso and Miró at the same time with the same cause, Republican Spain, at heart. In taking the destruction of Guernica as his subject Picasso chose an event of great emotional significance. The symbolism he used was directly inspired by the reality of the tragic bombardment and its victims taken by surprise during their daily occupations. *The Reaper*, although it is undoubtedly related to Miró's love of his native soil and its courageous people, is based on allusions that are detached from any precise person or event. Its appeal has a timeless dimension – a sense of space open to the ethereal voyage of the spirit beyond the limits of our material existence. The reality of Miró's painting exists in the dreams and desires of the imagination. His conception of reality is inseparable from his inner vision, nourished and made visible to us by his rare capacity to see clearly and to render faithfully that which he saw.

The fascination peculiar to the work of Miró lies above all in his power to extend our sense of reality. His purpose is to lead us to those realms of anonymity that transcend painting, an aim which became increasingly evident in the clarity and vigour of his later bursts of creativity. The persistence and integrity of his effort, and his willingness to renounce the exuberant charm of his earlier work, gave him the power he needed in his transcendental role as the seer who can take us with him into the highest regions of perception.

Epilogue

Eduardo de Benito

The dapper little man in a pinstripe suit and shiny black shoes, sitting beside me at the Marlborough Gallery in London one morning in 1966, was Joan Miró. 'The fork attacks the apple,' he said, 'as if it were a bayonet. The apple is Spain.'

66   He was explaining for my benefit the symbols in *Still-life with Old Shoe*, painted in 1937 at the beginning of the Spanish Civil War. As he did so it became apparent that the revulsion he felt for Fascism, still in power at that time in Spain, was a reality as tangible as the objects in his painting. Something *real* was needed to fight the hideous reality of oppression and injustice. In 1970, in a rather untypical gesture for such a private man, he joined Antoni Tàpies and other Catalan artists and intellectuals in a march to Montserrat Abbey to protest against the death sentences passed on several members of the Basque group ETA at the notorious Burgos trial.

From then on Miró appeared to be quite happy to let us know he was going to take notice more openly of the real world. He acknowledged, for instance, the oil crisis of 1973, and the sudden awareness that natural resources are finite, by enhancing the dominant role of black in his paintings and graphic work; symbolically, he was economizing in the use

141   of colour. His *Sobreteixims* (1973), a series of works on rough jute mats, would seem to indicate a positive reaction to the ecological ideas taking shape all around him, although some might prefer to interpret them as a return to his peasant roots: both interpretations, in any case, are compatible.

During that period – the early 1970s – he began to feel an urge for his message to reach a greater number of people, and, as a result, his graphic output increased dramatically. The colours were as radiant as ever, but they were now controlled by imposing, black surroundings, as in the lithographs

141 ABOVE *Sobreteixim-Sack 8*, 1973
142 OPPOSITE *Landscape*, 1974

The Amorous Bird (1973) or *Montroig III* (1973), or in paintings
like *Landscape* (1974), where a massive, black, trapezoidal shape
completely overwhelms a strip of green background. Miró's
blacks have been compared to his silences – the lack of colour
to the lack of sound, both serene and mysterious. The black,
however, reaches further, its impact being visual: a presence,
in the troubled world of his old age, rather than an absence.

Throughout the 1970s Miró worked with Artigas on ceramic
murals for public places. He designed one for IBM in Barcelona
in 1976, using a brush, a watering can and, sometimes, a bucket
to apply the black; and, in 1980 he finished the maquette for the
very large mural at the Palace of Congresses and Exhibitions
in Madrid.

143, 144 Scenes from
Mori el Merma, with La
Claca, Barcelona, 1978

Like Goya, and most great artists before him, he was anxious to go on learning until the end. In 1976 he collaborated with La Claca, an enthusiastic group of young Catalan actors, designing and painting for them a whole cast of biomorphic creatures headed by a grotesque and inimitable version of Alfred Jarry's Ubu Roi, who steps effortlessly into the shoes of the, then, recently dead Spanish dictator. The ensuing show, *Mori el Merma*, played to full houses in Majorca, Barcelona, the Pompidou Centre in Paris and Riverside Studios in London.

143, 144

At eighty-four, Miró used the technique of monotype for the first time; and two years later, in 1979, he produced his first stained-glass windows ever for the Fondation Maeght at Saint-Paul de Vence, where his sculptures welcome the visitor on the sun-drenched terraces of a Provençal garden. He then created a suite of drawings so that music could be composed around them for the ballet *L'Uccello Luce*, first performed at the Teatro La Fenice in Venice in 1981.

A year later, he gave us *Personnage*, an outer-space, warrior-like figure in bronze, who casts a sinister eye on Earth. An omen?

The old master was getting very frail, sustained only by the sight of the stars in the Mediterranean sky. On 25 December 1983, he finally reached for the stepladder, always close at hand, and climbed into the night of times, his beloved night.

Notes

Bibliographical details not given here will be found in the Bibliography

Preface

1 Roland Penrose, *Scrap Book 1900 to 1981* (London, Thames & Hudson, 1981), p. 36
2 Two letters and a postcard from Miró to Roland Penrose, held in private archive, UK
3 Penrose appointment diary for 27 March 1939. Roland Penrose Archives, National Galleries of Scotland, Edinburgh
4 Letter from Vidal to Penrose dated 1946. Roland Penrose Archives, National Galleries of Scotland, Edinburgh
5 https://collections.artsmia.org/art/6075/a-toute-epreuve-joan-miro
6 Coll. Fundació Joan Miró, Barcelona
7 Roland Penrose, *Scrap Book 1900 to 1981* (London, Thames & Hudson, 1981), p. 232
8 'Roland Penrose', an exhibition arranged by the Arts Council of Great Britain, opened at the Fermoy Gallery in Kings Lynn, Norfolk, 25 July to 9 August 1980, with a six-venue tour ending at Fundació Joan Miró, Barcelona, 26 February to 29 March 1981, with the support of the British Council

Chapter 1
A Period of Growth

1 Guillaume Apollinaire, *Les Peintres cubistes* (Geneva, Cailler, 1956), p. 36
2 *Ibid*
3 Dupin, *Miró*, p. 129 (132). All quotations from Dupin are Roland Penrose's own translations from the French original; page references to the English edition are given in parentheses
4 Dupin, *Joan Miró: la vie et l'oeuvre*, p. 76 (76)
5 *Ibid*., p. 129 (132)

Chapter 2
Paris and Surrealism

1 Sweeney, 'Joan Miró, Comment and Interview', p. 209
2 Breton, *Le Surréalisme et la peinture*, p. 94
3 *La Révolution surréaliste*, no. 3 (April 1925)
4 Miró, 'Je travaille comme un jardinier', p. 45
5 Miró, 'Je rêve d'un grand atelier', p. 25
6 Sweeney, *Joan Miró*, p. 13
7 Jean and Mezei, p. 154
8 Breton, *Le Surréalisme et la peinture*, p. 68
9 Sweeney, 'Joan Miró, Comment and Interview', p. 209
10 Hunter, p. xxxv
11 Herbert Read, *The Art of Jean Arp* (London, Thames & Hudson; New York, Abrams, 1968), p. 114
12 Hunter, p. xxx
13 Jean Arp, *Jours effeuillés* (Paris, Gallimard, 1968)
14 *La Révolution surréaliste*, no. 7 (June 1926)
15 *La Révolution surréaliste*, no. 8 (December 1926)
16 Paul Eluard, *A Toute épreuve* (Geneva, Gérald Cramer, 1958)
17 Waldberg, *Surrealism*, p. 41

Chapter 3
'Assassinate Painting!'

1 Duthuit, p. 261
2 *Ibid*
3 Breton, *Les Constellations*, pp. 10–11
4 Fitzsimmons (no page number)
5 Miró, 'Je travaille comme un jardinier', p. 49

Chapter 4
War and Isolation

1 Breton, *Les Constellations*, p. 8.
2 Hunter, p. xxix.
3 Breton, *Les Constellations*, p. 11.
4 Sweeney, 'Joan Miró, Comment and Interview', p. 211.
5 Hunter, pp. xxvi, xxix.
6 *Ibid*.

Chapter 5
New Horizons

1 Dupin, *Joan Miró: la vie et l'oeuvre*, p. 376 (382)
2 Miró, 'Je rêve d'un grand atelier', p. 25
3 Dupin, *Joan Miró: la vie et l'oeuvre*, p. 466 (482)

Chapter 6
Sculpture and Other Media

1 Bernier, p. 46
2 Dupin, *Joan Miró: la vie et l'oeuvre*, p. 384 (432)
3 *Ibid*., p. 444 (476)

Chapter 7
Poetry and Reality

1 This and subsequent quote, Miró, 'Je travaille comme un jardinier', pp. 39, 43 (translation adapted)

2 Dupin, *Joan Miró: la vie et l'oeuvre*, p. 432 (464)

3 Miró, 'Je travaille comme un jardinier', p. 44

4 *Ibid*., p. 43

5 *Ibid*., p. 39

6 Waldberg, 'Le Miromonde', p. 25

7 Miró, 'Je travaille comme un jardinier', p. 47

8 *Ibid*., p. 48

9 Mircea Eliade, *Myths, Dreams and Mysteries* (London, Collins, 1968), p. 62

10 *Ibid*., p. 125

11 Antonin Artaud, *Œuvres complètes* (Paris, Gallimard, 1967), VII, p. 24

12 Stéphane Mallarmé, *Œuvres complètes* (Paris, Gallimard, 1945), pp. 455, 477

13 R. D. Laing, *The Politics of Experience* (Harmondsworth, Penguin Books, 1967), p. 36

14 Miró, 'Je travaille comme un jardinier', p. 39

15 Charles Baudelaire, *The Mirror of Art* (London, Phaidon, 1955), p. 144

16 Max Jacob, *Correspondance* (Paris, Editions de Paris, 1953), 1, p. 31

Bibliography

Barr, Alfred H., Jr, ed. *Fantastic Art, Dada, Surrealism.* New York, Museum of Modern Art, 1936

Bernier, Rosamond. 'Miró céramiste'. *L'Œil*, no. 17 (May 1956)

Bonnefoy, Yves. *Miró.* Milan, Silvana Editoriale d'Arte, 1964

Breton, André. *Le Surréalisme et la peinture.* New York, Brentano's, 1945. This is a revised version of a text first published in *La Révolution surréaliste*, nos. 4, 6, 7, 9, 10 (1927)

——. *Les Constellations.* New York, Pierre Matisse Gallery, 1959

Cirici Pellicer, Alejandro. *Miró y la imaginación.* Barcelona, Omega, 1949

Dupin, Jacques. *Joan Miró: la vie et l'oeuvre.* Paris, Flammarion, 1961. English translation: *Joan Miró: Life and Work.* New York, Abrams; London, Thames & Hudson, 1962. Comprehensive bibliography by Bernard Karpel

——. *Miró.* Paris, UNESCO; London, Collins, 1962

Duthuit, Georges. 'Où allez-vous, Miró?'. *Cahiers d'Art*, vol. XI, nos. 8–10 (1936)

Erben, Walter. *Miró.* London, Lund Humphries, 1959

Fitzsimmons, James. *Miró – 'Peintures sauvages' 1934–53.* New York, Pierre Matisse Gallery, 1958

Gomis, Joaquim, and Joan Prats Vallés. *Atmósfera Miró* (with English translation). Barcelona, Ediciones Polígrafa, 1959. Preface by James Johnson Sweeney

——. *Creación Miró 1961* (with English translation). Barcelona, Ediciones Polígrafa, 1962. Preface by Yvon Taillandier

——. *Creación en el espacio de Joan Miró* (with English translation). Barcelona, Ediciones Polígrafa, 1966. Preface by Roland Penrose

Greenberg, Clement. *Joan Miró.* New York, Quadrangle Press, 1949

Hunter, Sam. *Joan Miró: His Graphic Work.* New York, Abrams, 1958

Jean, Marcel, and Arpad Mezei. *Histoire de la peinture surréaliste.* Paris, Editions du Seuil, 1959. English translation: *History of Surrealist Painting*, New York, Grove Press, 1960; London, Weidenfeld and Nicolson, 1962

Lassaigne, Jacques. *Miró.* Lausanne, Skira, 1963

Miró, Joan. 'Je rêve d'un grand atelier'. *XXᵉ Siècle*, vol. 1, no. 2 (1938), p. 25

——. 'Je travaille comme un jardinier. Propos recueillis par Yvon Taillandier' (with English translation by Joyce Reeves). *XXᵉ Siècle*, vol. X, no. 1 (1959)

Penrose, Roland. *Miró.* 'The Masters' series. Bristol, Purnell, 1965

Perucho, Juan. *Joan Miró y Cataluña* (with English translation). Barcelona, Ediciones Polígrafa, 1968

Prévert, Jacques, and Georges Ribemont-Dessaignes. *Joan Miró.* Paris, Maeght, 1956

Soby, James Thrall. *Joan Miró.* New York, Museum of Modern Art, 1959

Sweeney, James Johnson. *Joan Miró.* New York, Museum of Modern Art, 1941

——. 'Joan Miró, Comment and Interview'. *Partisan Review*, vol. xv, no. 2 (1948)

Waldberg, Patrick. *Surrealism.* London, Thames & Hudson; New York, McGraw-Hill, 1965

——. 'Le Miromonde'. *Derrière le miroir*, nos. 164–65 (April–May 1967), p. 25

Zervos, Christian, ed. 'L'Oeuvre de Joan Miró de 1917 à 1933'. *Cahiers d'Art*, vol. IX, nos. 1–4 (1934). Special number

List of Illustrations

Measurements are given in centimetres and inches, height before width before depth, where applicable

All works are by Joan Miró unless otherwise specified. All works by Joan Miró are © Successió Miró 2022

1 Joan Miró with the ceramic *Green Woman*, 1968. Photo Francesc Català-Roca/Successió Miró Archive
2 Joan Miró and Roland Penrose, Majorca, 1970 (photographed by Lee Miller). © Lee Miller Archives, England 2021. All rights reserved. leemiller.co.uk
3 Joan Miró, Dominique (Odette Lemort) Eluard and Roland Penrose looking at work plate for *A Toute épreuve* by Paul Eluard, Atelier Lacourière-Frélaut, Paris, 1956 (photographed by Lee Miller). © Lee Miller Archives, England 2021. All rights reserved. leemiller.co.uk
4 *Painting*, 1925. Oil on canvas, 88 × 116.4 (36¾ × 45⅞). Collection of Jake and Hélène Marie Shafran
5 Joan Miró modifying *Painting*, 1925, Farleys House, East Sussex, 1965 (photographed by Antony Penrose). Antony Penrose © Lee Miller Archives, England 2021. All rights reserved. leemiller.co.uk
6 Joan Miró signing Farleys Visitors' Book, Farleys House, East Sussex, 14 September 1964 (photographed by Antony Penrose). Antony Penrose © Lee Miller Archives, England 2021. All rights reserved. leemiller.co.uk
7 *Design for Desmond Morris*, 1964. Felt-tip pen and ball-point pen on the inside front cover of a book, 29.7 × 41.5 (11¾ × 16⅜). Private collection. Photo Christie's Images/Bridgeman Images
8 *Cornudella. Hermitage of Sant Joan del Codolar*, undated. Charcoal, sanguine and Conté crayon on paper, 14.6 × 21.9 (5¾ × 8⅝). Fundació Joan Miró, Barcelona (FJM 79a)

9 *Untitled (Snake)*, undated. Graphite pencil and charcoal on paper, 48.5 × 63 (19⅛ × 24⅞). Fundació Joan Miró, Barcelona (FJM 246)
10 *Untitled (Back of Nude)*, 1915. India ink and wash on paper, 31 × 21 (12¼ × 8⅜). Galerie Lelong, Zurich
11 *Untitled (Market Scene)*, 1915. Graphite pencil on paper, 22.5 × 31.8 (8⅞ × 12⅝). Fundació Joan Miró, Barcelona (FJM 232)
12 *Still-life with Knife*, 1916. Oil on canvas, 59.5 × 68.5 (23½ × 27). Nahmad collection, Monaco
13 *Siurana, the Path*, 1917. Oil on canvas, 60 × 73 (23⅝ × 28¾). Museo Nacional Centro de Arte Reina Sofía, Madrid
14 *Portrait of Enric Cristòfol Ricart*, 1917. Oil and pasted paper on canvas, 81.6 × 65.7 (32¼ × 25⅞). The Museum of Modern Art, New York. Florene May Schoenborn Bequest
15 *Standing Nude*, 1918. Oil on canvas, 152 × 122 (59⅞ × 48⅛). Saint Louis Art Museum. Friends Fund
16 *Nude with Mirror*, 1919. Oil on canvas, 113 × 102 (44½ × 40¼). Kunstsammlung Nordrhein-Westfalen, Düsseldorf. Photo Successió Miró Archive
17 *Portrait of a Young Girl*, 1919. Oil on paper on canvas, 35 × 27 (13⅞ × 10¾). Fundació Joan Miró, Barcelona. Gift of Joan Prats (FJM 4661)
18 *Self-portrait*, 1919. Oil on canvas, 73 × 60 (28¾ × 23⅝). Musée national Picasso, Paris
19 *The Vegetable Garden with Donkey*, 1918. Oil on canvas, 64 × 70 (25¼ × 27⅝). Moderna Museet, Stockholm. Purchase 1965 (The Museum of Our Wishes)
20 *Mont-roig, Vineyards and Olive Trees*, 1919. Oil on canvas, 72 × 90 (28⅜ × 35½). The Metropolitan Museum of Art, New York. Jacques and Natasha Gelman Collection, 1998. Photo The Metropolitan Museum of Art/Art Resource, NY/Malcolm Varon
21 *Horse, Pipe and Red Flower*, 1920. Oil on canvas, 82.5 × 75 (32½ × 29⅝). Philadelphia Museum of Art. Gift of Mr and Mrs C. Earle Miller, 1986
22 *The Table (Still-life with Rabbit)*, 1920. Oil on canvas, 130 × 110 (51¼ × 43⅜). Private collection. Photo Christie's Images Ltd/SuperStock
23 *The Farm*, 1921–22. Oil on canvas, 132 × 147 (52 × 57⅞). National Gallery of Art, Washington, DC. Gift of Mary Hemingway
24 *Interior (The Farmer's Wife)*, 1922–23. Oil on canvas, 81 × 65 (32 × 25⅝). Centre Pompidou, Paris. Photo Centre Pompidou, MNAM-CCI, Dist. RMN-Grand Palais/Jean-François Tomasian

25 *The Ploughed Field*, 1923–24. Oil on canvas, 66 × 92.7 (26 × 36½). Solomon R. Guggenheim Museum, New York
26 *Carnival of Harlequin*, 1924–25. Oil on canvas, 66 × 93 (26 × 36⅝). Albright-Knox Art Gallery, Buffalo, New York. Room of Contemporary Art Fund, 1940
27 *Dialogue of Insects*, 1924–25. Oil on canvas, 73 × 92 (28¾ × 36¼). Photo Bridgeman Images
28 *The Hunter (Catalan Landscape)*, 1923–24. Oil on canvas, 64.8 × 100.3 (25⅝ × 39½). The Museum of Modern Art, New York. Purchase, 1936
29 *Portrait of Madame K*, 1924. Charcoal, coloured crayon, pastel, sanguine, white chalk and pencil on primed (blanc de Meudon) canvas, 116.5 × 91 (45⅞ × 35⅞). Private collection
30 *The Family*, 1924. Charcoal, chalk and Conté crayon on flocked paper, 74.3 × 102.9 (29¼ × 40½). The Museum of Modern Art, New York. Gift of Mr and Mrs Jan Mitchell
31 *Maternity*, 1924. Oil on canvas, 92 × 73 (36¼ × 28¾). Scottish National Gallery of Modern Art, Edinburgh. Purchased with help from the National Heritage Memorial Fund, the Art Fund (William Leng Bequest) and members of the public, 1991. Photo National Galleries of Scotland/Bridgeman Images
32 *Head of a Catalan Peasant*, 1925. Oil and pencil on canvas, 92 × 73 (36¼ × 28¾). Tate Modern, London. Purchased jointly with the Scottish National Gallery of Modern Art with assistance from the Art Fund, the Friends of the Tate Gallery and the Knapping Fund 1999. Photo Tate
33 *Painting-Poem (Photo: This Is the Colour of My Dreams)*, 1925. Oil and hand-written inscription on canvas, 97 × 130 (38¼ × 51¼). The Metropolitan Museum of Art, New York. The Pierre and Maria-Gaetana Matisse Collection, 2002
34 *Head of a Pipe-smoker*, 1925. Oil on canvas, 64 × 49 (25¼ × 19⅜). Private collection. Photo John Webb (Brompton Studio)
35 *Painting*, 1925. Oil on canvas, 114.5 × 145.7 (45⅛ × 57⅜). The Solomon R. Guggenheim Foundation. Peggy Guggenheim Collection, Venice, 1976. Photo Bridgeman Images
36 *The Birth of the World*, 1925. Oil on canvas, 250.8 × 200 (98¾ × 78¾). The Museum of Modern Art, New York. Acquired through an anonymous fund, the Mr and Mrs Joseph Slifka and Armand G. Erpf Funds, and by gift of the artist
37 *The Policeman*, 1925. Oil on canvas, 248 × 195 (97¾ × 76⅞). Art Institute of Chicago. Bequest of Claire Zeisler. Photo Peter Barritt/SuperStock
38 *Painting-Poem (Le corps de ma brune puisque je l'aime comme ma chate habillée en vert salade comme de la grêle c'est pareil)*, 1925. Oil and hand-written inscription on canvas, 130 × 97 (51¼ × 38¼). Private collection. Photo Christie's Images/Bridgeman Images
39 *Painting-Poem (Un oiseau poursuit une abeille et la baisse)*, 1927. Oil, collage and hand-written inscription on canvas, 81 × 100 (32 × 39⅜). Private collection
40 *Painting-Poem (Amour)*, 1926. Oil and hand-written inscription on canvas, 146 × 114 (57½ × 45). Museum Ludwig, Cologne
41 *Painting-Poem (Le signe de la mort)*, 1927. Oil and hand-written inscription on canvas, 73 × 92 (28¾ × 36¼). Private collection. Photo Successió Miró Archive
42 *Dog Barking at the Moon*, 1926. Oil on canvas, 73 × 92 (28¾ × 36¼). Philadelphia Museum of Art. A. E. Gallatin Collection, 1952
43 *Person Throwing a Stone at a Bird*, 1926. Oil on canvas, 73 × 92 (28¾ × 36¼). The Museum of Modern Art, New York. Purchase, 1937
44 Hendrik Martenszoon Sorgh, *The Lute Player*, 1661. Oil on panel, 51.5 × 38.5 (20⅜ × 15¼). Rijksmuseum, Amsterdam
45 *Dutch Interior (I) (After Hendrik Maertensz Sorgh's The Lute Player)*, 1928. Oil on canvas, 92 × 73 (36¼ × 28¾). The Museum of Modern Art, New York. Mrs Simon Guggenheim Fund
46 *Potato*, 1928. Oil on canvas, 101 × 81.6 (39⅞ × 32⅛). The Metropolitan Museum of Art, New York. Jacques and Natasha Gelman Collection, 1998. Photo Bridgeman Images
47 *Portrait of Mistress Mills in 1750*, 1929. Oil on canvas, 116.7 × 89.6 (46 × 35¼). The Museum of Modern Art, New York. James Thrall Soby Bequest
48 *Portrait of a Dancer*, 1928. Painting-object with feather and hatpin, 100 × 81 (39⅜ × 32). Centre Pompidou, Paris. Gift of Mme Aube Breton Elléouët, 2003
49 *Collage*, 1929. Conté crayon, tar paper, paper, and flocked paper on paper, 101 × 66 (39⅞ × 26). Private collection
50 *Untitled. Drawing-collage*, 1933. Collage and Conté crayon on paper, 108 × 72 (42⅝ × 28⅜). Fundació Joan Miró, Barcelona. On loan from the Gallery K. AG. Photo Successió Miró Archive
51 *Torso of a Nude Woman*, 1931. Oil and watercolour on laid paper, 46.4 × 62.5 (18⅜ × 24⅝). Philadelphia Museum of Art. The Louise and Walter Arensberg Collection, 1950
52 *Seated Woman*, 1932. Oil on wood, 46 × 38 (18⅛ × 15). Private collection. Photo Bridgeman Images
53 *Painting*, 1933. Oil on canvas, 174 × 196.2 (68⅝ × 77¼). The Museum of Modern Art, New York. Loula D. Lasker Bequest (by exchange)

54 *Composition (Painting)*, 1933. Oil on canvas, 130 × 162 (51¼ × 63⅞). Národní Gallery, Prague. Photo Bridgeman Images

55 *Collage (Study for Painting, June 13, 1933)*, 1933. Cut-and-pasted photomechanical reproductions and graphite pencil on paper, 46.8 × 63 (18½ × 24⅞). The Museum of Modern Art, New York. Gift of the artist

56 *Preliminary collage for Painting 1933*, 1933. Graphite pencil and collage on paper, 47.2 × 63.2 (18⅝ × 25). Fundació Joan Miró, Barcelona (FJM 1296)

57 *Woman*, 1934. Pastel on paper, 106 × 71 (41¾ × 28). Private collection

58 *Persons in the Presence of Nature*, 1935. Oil and aqueous medium on cardboard, 75.6 × 105.7 (29⅞ × 41⅝). Philadelphia Museum of Art. The Louise and Walter Arensberg Collection, 1950

59 *The Farmers' Meal*, 1935. Oil on cardboard, 73 × 104 (28¾ × 41). Private collection

60 *The Two Philosophers*, 1936. Oil on copper, 35.6 × 49.8 (14 × 19⅝). Art Institute of Chicago. Gift of Mary and Leigh Block

61 *Two Personages in Love with a Woman*, 1936. Oil on copper, 26 × 34.9 (10¼ × 13¾). Art Institute of Chicago. Gift of Mary and Leigh Block. Photo The Art Institute of Chicago/Art Resource, NY

62 *Man and Woman in Front of a Pile of Excrement*, 1935. Oil on copper, 23 × 32 (9⅛ × 12⅝). Fundació Joan Miró, Barcelona. Gift of Pilar Juncosa de Miró (FJM 4676)

63 *Two Personages*, 1935. Oil, enamel, nails, ball bearings, cheesecloth, string and sand on cardboard, 104.3 × 71.4 (41 × 28⅛). The Kreeger Museum, Washington, DC

64 *Rope and People, I*, 1935. Oil on cardboard mounted on wood, with coil of rope, 104.8 × 74.6 (41¼ × 29⅜). The Museum of Modern Art, New York. Gift of the Pierre Matisse Gallery

65 *Painting*, 1936. Oil, casein, tar and pebbles on masonite, 78 × 108 (30¾ × 42⅝). Private collection

66 *Still-life with Old Shoe*, 1937. Oil on canvas, 81.3 × 116.8 (32⅛ × 46). The Museum of Modern Art, New York. Gift of James Thrall Soby

67 *The Reaper* in the stairwell of the Spanish Republican Pavilion at the Paris Exposition Internationale des Arts et Techniques dans la Vie Moderne, 1937. Oil on Celotex panels, 550 × 365 (216⅝ × 143¾). Unknown collection (lost). Photo Successió Miró Archive

68 *Aidez l'Espagne*, 1937. Pochoir with lithographic inscription on paper, 31.5 × 24.5 (12³⁄₁₀ × 9⅗). Editions Cahiers d'Art, Paris

69 *Painting-Poem (A Star Caresses the Breast of a Negress)*, 1938. Oil paint on canvas, 129.5 × 194.3 (51 × 76½). Tate. Purchased 1983. Photo Tate

70 *Portrait No. 1*, 1938. Oil on canvas, 163.2 × 130.2 (64¼ × 51¼). Baltimore Museum of Art. Bequest of Saidie A. May, BMA 1951.339. Photo Mitro Hood

71 *Head of a Woman*, 1938. Oil on canvas, 45.7 × 54.9 (18 × 21⅝). Minneapolis Institute of Art. Gift of Mr and Mrs Donald Winston. Photo Minneapolis Institute of Art/Bridgeman Images

72 *Seated Woman II*, 1939. Oil on canvas, 162 × 130 (63⅞ × 51¼). The Solomon R. Guggenheim Foundation. Peggy Guggenheim Collection, Venice, 1976. Photo Gianni Dagli Orti/Shutterstock

73 *Figure in Front of the Sea*, 1938. Oil on canvas, 61 × 50 (24⅛ × 19¾). Ikeda Museum of 20th Century Art, Shizuoka. Photo Successió Miró Archive

74 *Self-portrait I*, 1937–38. Pencil, crayon and oil on canvas, 146.1 × 97.2 (57⅝ × 38⅜). The Museum of Modern Art, New York. James Thrall Soby Bequest

75 *Self-portrait*, 1937–60. Oil and pencil on canvas, 146 × 97 (57½ × 38¼). Fundació Joan Miró, Barcelona. On loan from a private collection. Photo Bridgeman Images

76 *Self Portrait II*, 1938. Oil on burlap, 129.5 × 195.6 (51 × 77⅛). Detroit Institute of Arts. Gift of W. Hawkins Ferry. Photo Detroit Institute of Art/Bridgeman Images

77 *Flight of a Bird over a Plain II*, 1939. Oil on canvas, 81 × 100 (32 × 39⅜). Nahmad collection, Monaco

78 *Woman beside a lake whose surface has been made iridescent by a passing swan*, 1941/1959. Plate XVII from the Joan Miró/André Breton portfolio *Constellations*, 1959. Published by Pierre Matisse, New York. Pochoir reproduction after gouache, 43.3 × 35.8 (17⅛ × 14⅛). Centre Pompidou, Paris. Gift of Mme Maria-Gaetana Matisse, 1999. Photo Centre Pompidou, MNAM-CCI, Dist. RMN-Grand Palais/Audrey Laurans

79 *Pink twilight caresses the genitals of women and birds*, 1941. Gouache and oil wash on paper, 46 × 38 (18⅛ × 15). Private collection

80 *Women encircled by the flight of a bird*, 1941. Gouache and oil wash on paper, 46 × 38 (18⅛ × 15). Private collection

81 *The nightingale's song at midnight and morning rain*, 1940. Gouache and oil wash on paper, 38 × 46 (15 × 18⅛). Private collection

82 *People in the night guided by the phosphorescent tracks of snails*, 1940. Gouache and oil wash on

paper, 38 × 46 (15 × 18⅛). Philadelphia Museum of Art. The Louis E. Stern Collection, 1963

83 *Dancer Listening to the Organ in a Gothic Cathedral*, 1945. Oil on canvas, 197.1 × 130.6 (77⅝ × 51½). Fukuoka Art Museum

84 *Barcelona Suite IV*, 1944. Lithograph, 69.8 × 52.5 (27½ × 20¾). Harvard Art Museums/ Fogg Museum. Gift of the artist. Photo President and Fellows of Harvard College

85 *The Ladder of Escape*, 1940/1959. Plate II from the Joan Miró/André Breton portfolio *Constellations*, 1959. Published by Pierre Matisse, New York. Pochoir reproduction after gouache, 35.6 × 43.2 (14⅛ × 17⅛). Philadelphia Museum of Art. Gift of Ann E. and Donald W. McPhail, 2012

86 *Women and Bird in the Moonlight*, 1949. Oil paint on canvas, 81.3 × 66 (32⅛ × 26). Tate, Liverpool. Purchased 1951. Photo Tate

87 *The Blaze of the Sun Wounds the Lingering Star*, 1951. Oil and casein on canvas, 60 × 81 (23⅝ × 32)

88 *Composition with Strings*, 1950. Oil, plaster, rope on canvas, 99 × 76 (39 × 30). Van Abbemuseum, Eindhoven. Photo Peter Cox, Eindhoven

89 *Woman in Front of the Sun*, 1949. Oil on canvas, 116 × 89 (45¾ × 35⅛). Albertina, Vienna. The Batliner Collection CRP 862. Photo Album/ Oronoz/Superstock

90 *Painting*, 1953. Oil on canvas, 194.9 × 377.8 (76¾ × 148¾). Solomon R. Guggenheim Museum, New York. Photo The Solomon R. Guggenheim Foundation/Art Resource, NY

91 *Hope Comes Back to Us as the Constellations Flee*, 1954. Oil on canvas, 114 × 146 (45 × 57½). Private collection

92 *The Half-Open Sky Gives Us Hope*, 1954. Oil on canvas, 130 × 195 (51¼ × 76⅞). Fundació Joan Miró, Barcelona. On loan from the Gallery K. AG. Photo Successió Miró Archive

93 *Swallow Dazzled by the Flash of the Red Sloe*, 1925–60. Oil on canvas, 257 × 195 (101¼ × 76⅞). Private collection

94 *Woman and Bird II/X*, 1960. Oil on burlap, 65 × 61 (25⅝ × 24⅛). Collezione Fondazione Francesco Federico Cerruti per l'Arte. On long term loan, Castello di Rivoli Museo d'Arte Contemporanea, Rivoli-Torino. Photo Fondazione Francesco Federico Cerruti per l'Arte

95 *Solitude III/III*, 1960. Oil, gouache, crayon, pastel and ink on cardboard, 75 × 105 (29⅝ × 41⅜). Private collection. Courtesy Koller Auctions, Zurich

96 *Painting I/V*, 1960. Oil on canvas, 92 × 73 (36¼ × 28¾). Photo Galerie Maeght, Paris

97 *Painting II/V*, 1960. Acrylic and pastel on canvas, 92 × 73 (36¼ × 28¾). Fundació Joan Miró, Barcelona. On loan from the Gallery K. AG. Photo Successió Miró Archive

98 *The Red Disc*, 1960. Oil on canvas, 130 × 165 (51¼ × 65). The New Orleans Museum of Art. Bequest of Victor K. Kiam, 77.296

99 *Blue III*, 1961. Oil on canvas, 268 × 349 (105⅝ × 137½). Centre Pompidou, Paris. Purchase, 1988

100 *Words of the Poet*, 1968. Oil on canvas, 130.2 × 195 (51⅜ × 76⅞). Private collection. Photo Christie's Images/Bridgeman Images

101 *Poem III,* 1968. Oil on canvas, 205 × 174 (80¾ × 65⅝). Photo Galerie Maeght, Paris

102 *Letters and Numbers Attracted by a Spark (I)*, 1968. Acrylic on canvas, 146 × 114 (57½ × 45). Fundació Joan Miró, Barcelona (FJM 4716)

103 *Dance of People and Birds Against a Blue Sky; Sparks*, 1968. Oil on canvas, 173.6 × 291.6 (68⅜ × 114⅞). Centre Pompidou, Paris. On loan at Musée d'art moderne et contemporain, Saint-Etienne. Photo Centre Pompidou, MNAM-CCI, Dist. RMN-Grand Palais/image Centre Pompidou, MNAM-CCI

104 *The Gold of the Azure*, 1967. Acrylic on canvas, 205 × 173 (80¾ × 68⅛). Fundació Joan Miró, Barcelona (FJM 4699)

105 *Woman and Bird at Night*, 1968. Oil on canvas, 46 × 27 (18⅛ × 10¾). Photo Francesc Català-Roca

106 *Flight of Birds Encircling the Woman with Three Hairs During a Moonlit Night*, 1968. Oil on canvas, 92 × 73 (36¼ × 28¾). Private collection. Photo courtesy De Sarthe, Hong Kong

107 *Woman in Front of the Eclipse, her Hair Dishevelled by the Wind*, 1967. Oil on canvas, 243.2 × 194.6 (95¾ × 76⅝). Hirshhorn Museum and Sculpture Garden, Washington, DC. Museum Purchase with Funds Provided under the Smithsonian Institution Collections Acquisitions Program, 1980. Photo Lee Stalsworth

108 *Woman Encircled by a Flight of Birds in the Night*, 1968. Acrylic on tarpaulin (used for the grape harvest), 336 × 336 (132⅜ × 132⅜). Fundació Joan Miró, Barcelona (FJM 4715)

109 *Man and Woman*, 1931. Oil on wood, chain and pieces of metal, 34 × 18 × 5.5 (13½ × 7⅛ × 2¼). Centre Pompidou, Paris. Photo Centre Pompidou, MNAM-CCI, Dist. RMN-Grand Palais/Philippe Migeat

110 *Poetic Object*, 1936. Stuffed parrot on wood perch, stuffed silk stocking with velvet garter and doll's paper shoe suspended in hollow wood frame, derby hat, hanging cork ball,

celluloid fish and engraved map, 81 × 30.1 × 26 (31⅞ × 11⅞ × 10¼). The Museum of Modern Art, New York. Gift of Mr and Mrs Pierre Matisse

111 *Object of Sunset*, 1936. Painted wood (carob tree trunk), bed spring, gas burner, chain, shackle and string, 68 × 44 (26⅞ × 17⅜). Centre Pompidou, Paris. Purchase, 1975

112 *Figure and Bird*, 1968. Edition of seven. Bronze, 104 × 63 (41 × 24⅞). Photo Album/Oronoz/Superstock

113 *Figure*, 1968. Edition of four. Bronze, 55 × 50 (21¾ × 19¾). Cast by José Parellada, Barcelona

114 Joan Miró and Josep Llorens Artigas, *Woman*, 1968. Glazed ceramic, 172 × 70 × 28 (67¾ × 27⅝ × 11⅛). Private collection

115 Joan Miró and Josep Llorens Artigas, *Small Figure*, 1956. Stoneware, 21 × 7 (8⅜ × 2⅞). Private collection. Photo Francesc Català-Roca/Successió Miró Archive

116 Joan Miró and Josep Llorens Artigas, *Large Figure*, 1956. Earthenware, 100 × 35 × 33 (39⅜ × 13⅞ × 13). Kunsthaus Zürich. Gift of Gustav Zumsteg to the Zurich Art Friends, 1987. Photo Kunsthaus Zürich/Successió Miró Archive

117 Joan Miró and Josep Llorens Artigas, *Woman*, 1962. Earthenware, stoneware, iron and wood, 162 × 63 × 63.5 (63⅞ × 24⅞ × 25). Art Institute of Chicago. Mary and Leigh B. Block Foundation for acquisitions, 1967. Photo Successió Miró Archive

118 Joan Miró and Josep Llorens Artigas, *Green Woman*, 1968. Earthenware, 75 × 60 × 45 (29⅝ × 23⅝ × 17¾). Private collection. Photo Eric Pollitzer/Successió Miró Archive

119 *Mural Painting*, 1950–51. Oil on canvas, 192.1 × 596.9 (75¾ × 235). The Museum of Modern Art, New York. Mrs Simon Guggenheim Fund

120 Joan Miró and Josep Llorens Artigas, *Mural of the Moon*, 1957. Earthenware, 300 × 700 (118⅛ × 275⅝). UNESCO, Paris. Photo Francesc Català-Roca/Successió Miró Archive

121 Joan Miró and Josep Llorens Artigas, *Mural of the Sun*, 1957. Earthenware, 300 × 1500 (118⅛ × 590⅝). UNESCO, Paris. Photo Francesc Català-Roca/Successió Miró Archive

122 *Moon, Sun and a Star: Project for a Monument to Barcelona*, 1967/cast 1969. Bronze, 129.3 × 30 × 27.2 (51 × 11⅞ × 10¾). Hirshhorn Museum and Sculpture Garden, Washington, DC. The Joseph H. Hirshhorn Bequest, 1981

123 *The Arch*, 1963. Cement, 580 × 615 (228⅜ × 242¼). Fondation Maeght, Saint-Paul de Vence. Donated by the artist. Production funded by Marguerite and Aimé Maeght, 1964.

Photo Keystone-France/Gamma-Rapho via Getty Images

124 *The Pitchfork*, 1963. Iron and bronze, 507 × 455 (199⅝ × 179¼). Fondation Maeght, Saint-Paul de Vence. Donated by the artist. Production funded by Marguerite and Aimé Maeght, 1964. Photo Keystone-France/Gamma-Rapho via Getty Images

125 Plate from *Album 13*, 1948. Lithograph, 45 × 56 (17¾ × 22⅛). Private collection. Photo Denis Bloch Fine Art, Beverly Hills

126 *Small Engraving*, 1953. Engraving, 7 × 8 (2⅞ × 3¼). Location unknown

127 *The Great Magician*, 1968. Aquatint, etching, dry point and carborundum in colours, 89 × 67.5 (35⅛ × 26⅝). Private collection. Courtesy Swann Galleries

128 *In the Hail*, 1969. Aquatint in colours, sheet 62.8 × 89.5 (24⅝ × 35¼). Private collection. Published by Maeght Editeur, Paris. Courtesy Heritage Auctions

129 *The Calabash*, 1969. Etching and aquatint, sheet 101.6 × 68.6 (40 × 27⅛). Private collection. Published by Maeght Editeur, Paris. Courtesy Heritage Auctions

130 Cover for Tristan Tzara's *Parler seul*, 1948–50. Lithograph, 38.2 × 28.9 (15⅛ × 11½). Private collection. Published by Maeght Editeur, Paris

131 Camille Corot, *Château-Thierry, General View without the Tower of St-Crépin*, 1856 or 1863. Oil on canvas, 38 × 55.5 (15 × 21¾). Oskar Reinhart Collection 'Am Römerholz', Winterthur

132 *Homage to Corot*, 1967. Oil on canvas, 175 × 205 (69 × 80¾). Photo Francesc Català-Roca

133 Maquette for Barcelona airport mural, 1968–69. Gouache on paper, 100 × 500 (39⅜ × 196⅞). Fundació Joan Miró, Barcelona. Photo Jaume Blassi/Successió Miró Archive

134 *The lark's wing encircled with golden blue rejoins the heart of the poppy sleeping on the diamond-studded meadow*, 1967. Acrylic on canvas, 195 × 130 (76⅞ × 51¼). Fundació Joan Miró, Barcelona. On loan from the Gallery K. AG

135 *Silence*, 1968. Oil on canvas, 173.4 × 242.9 (68⅜ × 95¾). Centre Pompidou, Paris

136 *Nocturne*, 1938. Oil on cardboard, 54 × 73 (21⅜ × 28¾). Private collection

137 *Women and Bird in Front of the Moon*, 1944. Oil on burlap, 21.9 × 16.5 (8⅝ × 6½). The Baltimore Museum of Art. Bequest of Saidie A. May. Photo Mitro Hood

138 *Solar Bird*, 1966. Bronze, 121.9 × 180.3 × 101.6 (48 × 71 × 40). Art Institute of Chicago. Grant J. Pick Fund

139 *Lunar Bird*, 1966. Bronze, 118 × 177 × 102 (46½ × 69¾ × 40¼). Photo Ediciones Poligrafa SA

140 Joan Miró and Josep Llorens Artigas, *Woman and Bird*, 1962. Earthenware, 318 × 66 × 62 (125¼ × 26 × 24½). Fundació Pilar i Joan Miró a Mallorca. Donation of Successió Miró, 1993. Fundació Pilar i Joan Miró a Mallorca Photographic Archive

141 *Sobreteixim-Sack 8*, 1973. Acrylic, wool and felt on sackcloth, 172 × 160 (67¾ × 63). Fundació Joan Miró, Barcelona (FJM 7710)

142 *Landscape*, 1974. Oil on canvas, 215 × 173 (84¾ × 68⅛). Private collection

143, 144 Scenes from *Mori el Merma*, with La Claca, Barcelona, 1978. Photos Étienne Montes/ Gamma-Rapho via Getty Images

Index

The World of Art series is a comprehensive,
accessible, indispensable companion to the history
of art and its latest developments, covering themes,
artists and movements that span centuries and
the gamut of visual culture around the globe.

You may also like:

Abstract Art
Anna Moszynska

Mary Cassatt
Griselda Pollock

Cézanne
Richard Verdi

Dada
Hans Richter

Dalí
Dawn Ades

Marcel Duchamp
Dawn Ades, Neil Cox and
David Hopkins

Fauvism
Sarah Whitfield

Monet
James H. Rubin

Photomontage
Dawn Ades

World of Art

For more information about
Thames & Hudson, and the World of Art
series, visit **thamesandhudsonusa.com**